AN INTRODUCTION TO CONCURRENCY USING occam

ASPECTS OF INFORMATION TECHNOLOGY

This series is aimed primarily at final year undergraduate and postgraduate students of Electronics and Computer Science, and provides an introduction to research topics in Information Technology which are currently being translated into teaching course material. The series aims to build bridges between foundation material covered in the first two years of undergraduate courses and the major research topics now attracting interest within the field of IT.

The format of the series is deliberately different from that of typical research reference works within the fields of interest. Depth of coverage is restricted in favour of providing a readable and comprehensible introduction to each topic, and to keep costs within the requirements for a course textbook. Nevertheless, each book provides a comprehensive overview and introduction to its subject, aimed at conveying the key elements in an attractive and clear fashion.

Each chapter is terminated by a summary itemizing the key points contained within, and problems and exercises are provided where appropriate to enable the student to test his knowledge. For the serious student, each book contains a comprehensive further reading list of texts and key reference papers covering the field, as well as giving an indication of those journals which publish within the area.

Series editors: **A. C. Downton** *University of Essex*
R. D. Dowsing *University of East Anglia*

INTRODUCTION TO CONCURRENCY USING occam

R. D. Dowsing
School of Information Systems
University of East Anglia

VNR International

First published in 1988 by
Van Nostrand Reinhold (International) Co. Ltd
11 New Fetter Lane, London EC4P 4EE

Typeset in Times 10/12 pt by Columns of Reading

Printed in Great Britain by
T.J. Press (Padstow) Ltd., Padstow, Cornwall

ISBN 0–278–00059–2

British Library Cataloguing in Publication Data
Dowsing, R. D. (Roy D.)
Introduction to concurrency using occam
1. Computer systems. Operating systems.
Concurrent programming
I. Title
005.4′2

ISBN 0–278–00059–2

CONTENTS

PREFACE

The development of digital computers and computing, until recently, has been based largely on the pioneering work of Von Neumann in the 1940s. This has limited developments to sequential programming models. The main hardware developments during this period have been in the methods and techniques of improving the speed, size and performance of the computer. Due to vast improvement in technology the digital computer of today is several orders of magnitude more powerful than those of thirty years ago. Advances in software over the same period have concentrated on making the computer easier to use by the development of high level languages and operating systems.

In the last ten years or so attention has turned on the possibilities of utilizing concurrency in the higher levels of system architecture, for example, multiple processor systems and their associated software. Concurrency is already present at the lower levels of architecture, for example, collections of logic elements act as a set of concurrent bit processors. The reason for introducing concurrency into an architecture is usually one of the following: performance improvement, fault tolerance or extensibility. If several operations are performed concurrently then there is potentially a saving in time over performing them separately. If the same operation is performed by several processors concurrently then any faults in the hardware can be overcome by taking the majority result. Incrementally increasing the power of a computer by simply adding more processors should be cheaper than designing a range of machines with differing performance, hence another desire for using concurrency.

Although driven by these reasons, the development of concurrent computing has not proved to be as simple as some people expected. Although operating systems have existed for many years the development of application specific concurrent systems appears to require considerable training and intellectual effort and this book attempts to distil some of the problems and their solutions to give the reader a view of some of the field of concurrent computing. We cannot cover the whole field in such a book and we do not attempt to do so, rather we concentrate on a particular concurrent programming model and show, through the language occam®, some of the communication strategies to use in communicating processes. We illustrate these strategies through a number of examples and have chosen the language occam since it is simple and elegant with a well defined semantics. Furthermore, it has been attracting increasing interest with the expanding use of transputers.

These notes are intended to supplement a course on Systems Architecture and Concurrency Concepts. They assume that the reader is familiar with standard sequential programming concepts and has designed and implemented programs in a high-level language such as Pascal. This book is not intended to be a teaching text on occam; such texts are beginning to appear and some are referenced in the references. Rather this book uses a substantial part – in fact nearly all – of the occam language to illustrate some of the features of concurrency and some of the problems. Readers who work their way through the examples and exercises will acquire a good knowledge of the occam language.

THE PLAN OF THIS BOOK

In Chapter 1 we introduce some of the ideas of concurrent processing and relate them to the notions of sequential programming with which we assume the reader is familiar. Many of the ideas relating to concurrency have come out of work on operating systems and this chapter is a broad overview of some of the important topics which would be covered in an operating systems course. In this chapter we introduce some of the concepts of concurrency which are illustrated in the rest of the book by means of the programming language occam.

Chapter 2 introduces the language occam, designed at Inmos Ltd., which is a low-level concurrent programming language. We use this language as the basis of examples used in these notes. In Chapter 3 we introduce the basic schemes of communication and show how these schemes can be modelled in occam for a single reader and a single writer. Chapter 4 extends these communication primitives to allow for multiple readers and writers. Chapter 5 looks at two general techniques for communicating between a set of readers and writers and Chapter 6 extends these ideas to distributed systems where processes are physically distributed.

Chapter 7 is a case study of the simulation of digital systems using occam, giving an example of the use of occam in a large program and illustrating some good and bad points in the language. This is followed by a chapter describing the use of concurrent processing concepts in modelling data structures. The following chapter, Chapter 9, takes as an example the design of a simplified operating system using the occam programming language. The penultimate chapter, Chapter 10, uses occam to show how concurrency can be applied to real-time systems, whilst Chapter 11 examines the need for higher level communication primitives and describes some possible models and the improvements they bring.

Much of this text has been used for teaching a course on Systems Architecture and Concurrency to second and third year undergraduates. I would like to thank all the staff and students associated with this course, especially Professor Schuman and Ralph Elliott, for their help and insight in producing this text. Any remaining errors are, of course, solely my responsibility.

1

FROM SEQUENTIALITY TO CONCURRENCY

As a prelude to the main topic of the book we first consider some of the fundamental notions in concurrency and define some of the terms we will use later. Firstly, we will define concurrency. Two actions are said to be concurrent if they overlap in time. Generalizing from the sequential world would therefore appear on the surface to be simply a matter of adding some constructs to the language or notation to specify that two or more actions may overlap in time. Whilst this is true at the superficial level, there are more major problems at the conceptual level. Allowing for the fact that concurrency changes the timing relationship between actions, we can no longer speak of just 'before' and 'after' relationships between actions; we need many more covering all the possible types of overlap. This creates all sorts of problems when reasoning about concurrent systems. We shall encounter some of these problems later in this chapter and throughout the book.

Of necessity this chapter is rather brief and concise on some topics. Some readers may wish to re-read this chapter after reading the rest of the book to place the occam examples given there in context.

1.1 PROCESSES

The fundamental concept underlying the study of concurrency is that of the **process** (Horning and Randell, 1973) and we shall spend some time here exploring this concept in detail.

In the normal sequential programming world a process is equated with a program in execution. This is a rather loose definition; it is better to think of a process as being characterized by:

a a **context** or **environment**;
b a set of **actions** which operate within that context.

The context is characterized by:

a a set of **definitions**, called the **namespace**;
b a set of **resources**, sometimes called the **statespace**.

In terms of a sequential program the context is the environment of the program, both the names and the variables which hold the state of the program at any one time, and the action is simply the code of the program. Only one instruction at a time may be executed in a process, thus a process is strictly sequential.

There are two distinct entities which may be referred to in a process. Firstly, there is the **template** from which the process is created which consists of the code and the environment of the process. In terms of our example this is the program, that is, the text including the definitions of the variables required and the code for the actions. Secondly, there is an **instance** of the process which is an execution of the process code in its environment. In our example this is the execution of the program.

An instance of a process has temporal properties; it is created, it lives and it dies. A static system is one in which the number of processes is known before execution time, whilst a dynamic system is one in which the number of processes changes as execution proceeds and normally depends on input data. As might be expected the latter case is more flexible but requires greater management overheads.

As the execution of a process proceeds there is a change of state, represented by a change in the environment of the process. Thus the state of the process at any instant in time can be characterized by the current context and by the current position reached in executing the code of the process.

In the discussion above we have treated a program as an example of a process but we could think of each block in a program as a separate process since the environment can change on entering a block and the code for that block can be thought of as implementing an action. Thus each function or procedure can also be thought of as a process and a program can be considered as a set of processes rather than as a single process. In fact, in occam, the language we shall use for examples in the rest of this book, the basic unit of the language is a process which corresponds to a statement in a typical sequential programming language. In the same way that simple statements can be combined to form composite statements in a typical sequential programming language so simple processes can be combined to form composite processes in the concurrent world.

Thus we can model a program as a collection of processes, each of which is sequential. The distinguishing feature of the sequential programming world is that only one of the processes is active at any one instant in time. For example, if we consider a sequential program consisting of a number of procedures to be a collection of processes, each one being the execution of a procedure, then only one of the processes will be in execution at any one time since in the sequential programming model any procedure which calls another procedure is itself suspended until the called procedure terminates.

In a concurrent system there are multiple processes potentially active at the same time. We shall consider the implementation of processes later in this chapter but we must make clear here the difference between a sequential set of processes and a concurrent set of processes. In the former case there is a defined order of execution of the processes, for example, in a sequential program the order of execution of the procedures is defined in the code. In the case of a concurrent set of processes there is no ordering defined and so the ordering of execution is immaterial, that is, the processes may be executed in any order . For example, if processes P1 and P2 and P3 are a concurrent set of processes then they could be executed sequentially in any one of the following orders:

P1;P2;P3
P1;P3;P2
P2;P1;P3
P2;P3;P1
P3;P1;P2
P3;P2;P1

where ';' represents the sequential ordering operator. At the other extreme they could be executed in parallel, that is:

P1 || P2 || P3

where || is the parallel operator. Alternatively they could be executed in any combination in between, such as P1 and P2 executing together and P3 being executed afterwards or even P1 starting and then P2 and P3 starting before P1 finishes, that is, overlap of the execution of P1 with P2 and P3. Thus concurrent execution is a relaxation of any ordering constraints. A further feature of a concurrent set of processes is that they are usually assumed to be asynchronous, that is, the execution speed of any one of the processes is independent of any of the others. As we shall see later the fact that they are asynchronous means that they have to be synchronized if they wish to communicate.

So far we have implied that processes require a Central Processing Unit (CPU) in order to be executed. However, an input–output device may be thought of as a processor since it obeys instructions to input or output data to and from the computer. Furthermore it operates asynchronously of the CPU and hence input–output operations may occur concurrently. Thus even a single CPU computer may allow multiple processes to be in operation concurrently, as indeed most operating systems do.

1.2 RESOURCES

Processes normally manipulate some form of data, but they may also, for example, read from, or write to, input–output devices. The generic term for things which may be manipulated by processes is **resource**.

Resources may be classified into two types, **dedicated** and **global**. Dedicated resources are effectively local to a process which means that there will be no contention for that resource. As we shall see later in this chapter and in the rest of the book, many of the techniques of sharing resources attempt to give the processes involved dedicated resources so that they may run concurrently rather than having some ordering constraint imposed on them due to contention for resources. Shared resources are necessarily global and give rise to dependent processes either implicitly or explicitly.

The two major types of sharable resource are **serially reusable resources** and **dynamically shared resources**. This latter type may be further subdivided into three sub-groups; **partitioned**, **multiplexed** and **interleaved**, with interleaving either real or virtual.

A typical example of a serially reusable resource is a line printer. When a process wishes to use a printer it must have exclusive use of the printer for the duration of its use since it does not want its output interspersed with another process's output. When the process has finished with the printer that resource may be allocated to another process. The process of allocation and deallocation, that is, resource management, is normally carried out by an operating system (Deitel, 1983) and is one of its major tasks. A simple printer management policy is for the operating system to allocate the printer to a process for that processes lifetime. This is rather wasteful since the process will only print for a small proportion of this time. A better method is for the process to inform the operating system when it wishes to use the printer by issuing acquire and release requests. The operating system may then allocate the printer resource depending on these requests. This indicates a facet called the grain of concurrency. In the case of the allocation of the printer for a process lifetime there is no concurrency possible if only one printer is available, assuming each process requires a printer, but with the use of the acquire and release primitives many processes can be active at once provided that only one of them requires the printer at any time. Here the unit of work is a section of the program, either requiring a printer or not, rather than the whole program. Similarly the same technique is often used in concurrent systems which share resources in order to improve the amount of concurrency. Multiple resources may be managed by the same techniques as single resources and hence an operating system normally deals with sets of processes requesting sets of resources.

In the case of **dynamically partitioned resources**, a good example of which is a disc sub-system, many processes can share different parts of the same resource concurrently. In the disc example, a disc may be subdivided into several file systems and a separate process may use each file system concurrently. If, instead of using separate files, processes need to share the same file, for example, if the same database is to be interrogated, then it may or may not be possible for the file to be accessed concurrently depending on a number of factors. If processes all share the same file concurrently, that is, the file is regarded as a **dynamically multiplexed resource**, then they must only be allowed read only access, otherwise corruption of the database could occur if two processes attempted to write at once. If processes wish to share a file and some of them wish to update the information then any updating must be performed in mutual exclusion to any other access to the file, that is two concurrent requests, if one is to update the file, have to be serialized. This type of file is called **dynamically interleaved resource**. We will consider this in more detail later in this chapter.

As stated previously, concurrent processes may share resources, for example, a set of programs may share a disc on a computer. There are several ways in which a resource may be shared. For example, a disc could be partitioned into several different partitions and each process could be given access to only a single partition. In effect this removes the sharing at this level although the communication route to the disc is still probably shared. This type of sharing is relatively easy to organize. There are many cases where sharing is required, for example, in an airline booking system two passengers trying to book seats on the same flight need access to the same data structure containing details of the present seat allocation. Thus there are cases where sharing has to be performed and this is much more difficult to organize. Consider the airline booking system again. The obvious restriction of access to the data structure is that only one process should be allowed to write to the structure at once otherwise the results will be unpredictable. However there is a further restriction. The normal way in which a booking is carried out is that the data structure is interrogated to see if there are any seats free and then, if there are suitable ones free, the structure is updated to reflect the fact that a number of seats have been sold. This series of transactions may fail, however, if another enquiry overlaps with it. Consider the case where travel agent A asks for the number of seats free and receives the reply 3. Another travel agent B enquires and is again given the answer 3. If B then books the 3 seats A will find that he is unable to book any although he has been told that there are 3 free. To overcome problems such as this elaborate mechanisms are necessary as explained later in this chapter.

We have thus modelled our concurrent system as a set of processes which manipulate a set of resources. We can regard the processes as active and the resources as passive, that is, the resources only respond to actions initiated by a process. However, we could think of our resources as being encapsulated in a process and hence make the only abstraction in our model a process. This has attractions as it reduces the number of different types of object in our model. We can still implement the active–passive roles if we wish since any process can wait for communication from any other process before proceeding, as we shall later in this chapter. We assume that the only entities in our system are processes for the rest of the discussion in this chapter.

1.3 PROCESS IMPLEMENTATION

Up until now we have been considering processes in the abstract but to execute a process the minimum physical resources required are a processor and memory. The processor executes the code and the memory stores the code and maintains the environment. A set of sequential processes can be mapped on to a single processor using the appropriate ordering constraints. In the case of a set of independent programs an operating system is normally responsible for organizing the ordering. Since the programs are logically independent the operating system can schedule them in any order it wishes and the order is usually determined by factors such as the program's priority, the number and type of resources it requires and the time it was submitted to the operating system. The multiplexing of many programs or jobs on to a single processor is known as **multi-programming**. In the case of a single program comprised of a set of procedures the ordering of execution of the procedures is completely defined and they have to be executed in this order. The execution of a concurrent set of processes on a computer system comprising of a number of processors is known as **multi-processing**. In this case it may be possible to assign each process to a separate processor but in general processors are a scarce resource and so the processors have to be shared among the processes.

There are several reasons for wishing to implement concurrent processes on more than one processor. The most obvious reason is to increase the performance of the system, that is, to execute the processes in as short a period of time as possible. The number of processes which can be executed concurrently depends on the ordering constraints of the processes and on the number of processors available at execution time. Another reason for wishing to implement processes concurrently is to obtain a measure of fault tolerance. If, instead of running a single process on a single processor, several copies are run on different processors then errors in the processors can be eliminated by accepting the results of the majority. Similarly, errors in the code can be eliminated by running copies of different code to perform the same function. A further reason for using multiple processor implementation is to provide a simple route to up-grade the performance of a computer system. In a multi-processor system to up-grade the performance more processors can be added to the system thus allowing more processes to be run concurrently. This is in contrast to the situation for sequential systems where the processor has to be replaced to obtain higher performance.

1.4 PROCESS COMMUNICATION

If processes are to co-operate, for example, to preserve some ordering constraint or as part of a larger task, they need to communicate. Processes may communicate in one of two ways. The simplest way is for them to share some address space and then any change made by a process can be seen directly by other processes sharing the address space. There are problems in this approach as discussed for dynamically shared resources above. For example, the actions of the processes have to be co-ordinated so that at most one writes at once. The second approach is for the processes to send messages to one another, either directly or indirectly. In this case the processes have non-overlapping address spaces and some communication sub-system has the task of passing messages between the communicating processes. In order to communicate directly the processes involved need to be synchronized so that the receiver is ready to receive when the sender is ready to send. This is known as **synchronous communication**. Alternatively, one or more buffers need to be inserted in the communication path to decouple the sender and receiver. This is known as **asynchronous communication**. The former case, used in the occam language (Inmos Ltd., 1984), implies no buffering in the communication system and the sender and receiver are held in synchronization until the data communication has taken place. In the asynchronous case the sender may deposit the data in the buffer and continue processing provided that there is space available in the buffer. If no space is available then the sender has to wait until a receiver removes a message, that is, the sender and receiver are synchronized when the buffer is full. Hence in asynchronous communication the sender and receiver proceed at their own rate provided that the buffer is not full.

Using these two basic communication schemes it is possible to build up more complicated ones. For example, the programming language

Ada (Ada, 1982) uses a form of synchronous communication called **rendezvous** which is described in more detail in a later chapter.

1.5 PROCESS NAMING

One model of communication involves processes sending messages to one another for communication. A question then arises as to how the recipient is named. One possibility is for the named communication channels to be named and processes to read and write to one or more of these named channels. This is the method used in the occam programming language illustrated in the rest of this book. Another method is for the destination process's identity to be quoted when the message is sent. The underlying message passing system is then responsible for delivering the message to the correct destination. Similarly the message will only be delivered when the destination requests a message from that source. This is equivalent to establishing a direct bidirectional link between the two processes:

send(P_2,message)
receive(P_1,message).

Similarly the receiver may elect to receive input from anywhere, the client-server model, in which case the receiver need not name the sender but can receive his identity.

send(P2,message)
receive(id,message).

The problem with these schemes is that the sender and receiver have to know details of the other processes in the system, specifically their names. To overcome this a named buffer may be inserted into the communication path so that processes now only have to be aware of the buffer name rather than the other process in the system. This type of buffer is often called a **mailbox**. Senders and receivers communicate by sending messages to the appropriate mailbox.

send(mb1,message)
receive(mb1,message).

This still leaves the problem of mailbox identity to be communicated to each process but this can be dealt with at process creation time or dynamically by the operating system. The mailbox may be used by any number of senders and receivers and hence one to many, many to one and many to many communication schemes can be implemented. To preserve the integrity of the messages, exclusive access to the mailbox by a single sender or receiver is normally enforced since the action of adding a message to the mailbox or removing one modifies the message storage structure.

1.6 SYNCHRONIZATION

One of the major problems in synchronization is maintaining the integrity of shared data. This manifests itself in the use of **critical regions** (Dijkstra, 1965; Hoare, 1972; Brinch Hansen, 1972) in programming. Critical regions are portions of code which may only be executed by a single process at a time. Using a bounded buffer as an example, the typical algorithm for the producer and consumer processes would be:

```
producer                          consumer

repeat forever                    repeat forever

produce next value                while buffer empty wait
                                  get value from buffer
while buffer full wait            update buffer count
insert value into buffer
update buffer count               consume value
```

If both the producers and consumers are able to read and write the count simultaneously then unpredictable actions could occur. For example, if the buffer was full and a consumer process removed a message, multiple producers could sense this and attempt to insert values into the buffer simultaneously, thus causing overwriting and values to be lost or buffer overflow and storage corruption. The simplest solution to the problem is to only allow a single process to manipulate the buffer at any one time; this is **mutual exclusion** (Dijkstra, 1965). Solutions to the mutual exclusion problem have not just to implement mutual exclusion but have to ensure that the scheduling of processes through a critical region is both efficient and fair.

Many solutions to this type of synchronization problem have been suggested. Whilst it is possible to program solutions to the bounded buffer discussed above using conventional programming techniques and flags programming the synchronization requirements of more complex problems is very difficult. Dijkstra (Dijkstra, 1965) was the first person to suggest a new type of synchronization tool called a **semaphore**. A semaphore is a global variable to which access is only allowed through the use of two atomic operations called P and V. The V operation increments the semaphore by 1 and the P operation decrements it by 1, providing that the semaphore is positive. If the semaphore is not positive then the P operation is delayed until the semaphore becomes positive. Both of these operations are atomic, that is, they cannot be interrupted so that manipulation of the semaphore by a single process at a time is guaranteed. Programming critical sections is now simple since all that is required to provide mutual exclusion is for a V(sem) to be inserted before the critical section and a P(sem) after it, with the value of sem initially set to 1. Other forms of synchronization are readily implemented by semaphores, for example to synchronize two processes so that one starts after another the first process sets a semaphore, V(sem), before it finishes and the second has P(sem) as its first statement. The problem with semaphores is that they are at too low a level for normal use in programming; it is very easy to make mistakes when programming with them and very difficult to debug programs which use them. In the same way that structured programming made writing and debugging sequential programs easier by removing the use of goto statements so a better tool for synchronization was required. One tool which emerged as a better way to write critical sections was by the use of a **monitor**.

A monitor (Brinch Hansen, 1973; Hoare, 1974) is a shared program unit, a module, which only allows a single process to execute it at any one time. It is based on the idea of abstract data types where a data structure is encapsulated with the routines to manipulate the structure. The monitor acts as a critical region but an extra mechanism, called a condition, is provided so that programmers can specify their own synchronization via condition variables. The only operations allowed on condition variables are **wait** and **signal**. Any process invoking a wait operation on a condition variable is suspended until another process invokes a signal operation on the same condition variable. A signal operation resumes only one suspended process and if there are no suspended processes no action is taken. Since only one process may be active inside a monitor at any time a process resuming another by a signal operation must either wait until the resumed process has exited the monitor or is waiting on another condition variable or the resumed process must wait until the awakening process has exited the monitor or waits on a condition variable. Different implementations of monitors have adopted different approaches.

Many more synchronization schemes have been suggested but space prevents their discussion here, except for **path expressions** (Campbell and Habermann, 1974). Based on the same ideas of abstract data types, path expressions express the synchronization constraints for external access to the operations on the encapsulated data. Several different types of path expression have been proposed, some based on regular expressions. One type of path expression not based on regular expressions, called open paths, has been incorporated into Pascal and the language used for programming concurrent applications. In this notation the path expression defines restrictions on the ordering of access to the operations on the data. The ':' operator specifies restrictions on concurrency, for example 2:read implies that a maximum of two invocations of read may be active simultaneously. The ';' operator specifies sequencing, for example write;read specificies that a write operation must precede each read operation. The ',' operator specifies selection, for example 1:(write,read) specifies that the read and write operations are mutually exclusive. This type of synchronization is at a higher level than monitors and condition variables but it is not clear whether it has the same power.

1.7 DEADLOCK

When a number of processes compete for a limited number of resources situations can arise where two or more processes cannot proceed since each requires resources already claimed by another blocked process. This is known as **deadlock** (Holt, 1972). There are two different strategies for dealing with deadlock, firstly to stop it happening and, secondly, to recover when it has happened.

As an example consider two cars proceeding in opposite directions along a single track road. When they meet deadlock has occurred since neither can proceed further. One recovery operation, called **rollback**, is for one of the cars to reverse backwards until a piece of road is reached where the cars can pass. This is equivalent to going back to a previous position for the car involved. In order for deadlock to be avoided the cars have to communicate via an agreed protocol before entering the single track road. This would normally be done by the use of traffic lights apportioning time to cars from different directions. Another scheme is similar to that used on railways where trains on a single track carry the key to unlock the use of the single track with them thus ensuring mutual exclusion of the use of the line.

Deadlock can only occur if the following four conditions hold simultaneously:

1. A circular wait is involved, for example, A is waiting for a resource from B which is waiting for a resource from C which is waiting for a resource from A.
2. At least one process is waiting to acquire additional resources whilst holding at least one other resource.
3. At least one of the resources involved is non-shareable.
4. Pre-emption is not allowed, that is, resources are retained by a process until it has finished with them.

There are a number of well-known algorithms for avoiding deadlock. The simplest of these is that all processes have to acquire all the resources they require as a single acquisition. Thus, if some of the resources are not available when requested the process does not acquire any of them and has to reissue the acquire request at a later time. Another algorithm allocates unique identification numbers to each resource. Processes may only request resources in increasing identification number order. Perhaps the best known deadlock avoidance algorithm is the Bankers Algorithm (Dijkstra, 1965; Habermann, 1969) which avoids deadlock by determining, at every resource request, whether the requested allocation could possibly lead to deadlock and, if so, refusing the request. This implies that the algorithm knows the exact resource requirements of each process in the system. A simple example of the Bankers Algorithm is presented in Chapter 7.

1.8 SCHEDULING

Whenever a number of clients compete to use a number of resources a scheduler or arbitrator is required to decide in which order requests are to be satisfied. In order to make this selection the scheduler has to have some criteria built in for discriminating amongst the clients. Some typical criteria which are used are first-come-first-served, highest priority next and round robin.

We are not so much interested here in the algorithms but more in the problems which arise in applying them. One of these problems, which arises particularly with priority schemes, is starvation. In a system which is constantly overloaded, that is, there are always outstanding resource requests, some low priority clients may never be scheduled since there are always higher priority requests outstanding. One solution is to increase a client's priority with time so that eventually the client will gain a high enough priority to run. Another problem in scheduling concerns the timing of scheduling operations. Because of the inherent asynchronism in the system, clients progress at their own rate, there is no overall view of time and hence when the scheduling operation is performed there is no guarantee that any particular timing will be observed.

SUMMARY

In this chapter we have outlined the major topics of concurrency, such as sharing, synchronization, communication and scheduling based on the notion of a concurrent system as a set of communicating sequential processes. The reason for using concurrency in a system is usually to improve its performance although concurrency may also be used to provide a measure of fault tolerance and to provide the basis for an extensible computer system where the performance of the computer may be enhanced by adding more processors rather than replacing the processor. In the rest of this book we shall use the concurrent language occam to illustrate some of the principles and problems of concurrency, concentrating initially on the communication between processes.

2

INTRODUCTION TO occam

In this chapter we introduce the language occam (Inmos Ltd., 1984), a programming language developed at Inmos Ltd. as the lowest level language for programming a transputer or array of transputers. A transputer may be thought of as a powerful microprocessor with a number of inbuilt fast serial communication interfaces, currently four in number. The transputer was designed with occam in mind so it is designed to effectively implement the constructs of the language. Occam is a descendant of Communicating Sequential Processes (CSP) designed by C. A. R. Hoare (Hoare, 1978), although this name is now reserved for the theory underlying the language (Hoare, 1985). The main difference between occam and standard sequential programming languages is that occam allows the user to create autonomous processes which can communicate with one another via input and output over named channels.

There are actually two different languages referred to as occam; the original language usually known simply as occam which is defined in (Inmos Ltd., 1984) and a later development called occam 2 which has considerable differences from the original language. We have used the original language in this book since it is still the most widely available at present. The major differences between the two languages are given in an appendix and an Inmos tutorial on occam 2 should be published shortly.

In this brief introduction only the basic ideas in occam are explained and a few examples given; case studies of more substantial examples are given in later chapters. It is assumed that the reader is familiar with a typical high-level language such as Pascal and can therefore read a typical occam program without much difficulty. Readers who require more details of the language should consult the language manual (Inmos Ltd., 1984). There are several implementations of occam available on a range of different computers and some, especially those not produced by

Inmos Ltd., do not conform exactly to the language described in the reference manual. As far as we are aware the programs described in this book do conform to the reference manual except where stated.

2.1 THE LANGUAGE MODEL

The model of computation supported by occam is a set of **processes** which communicate with each other over named communication **channels**. An occam process is similar to a statement in a standard sequential programming language. For example, the assignment statement x:= 0 in Pascal has a direct analogue in occam; the process x := 0. The difference between the concept of statement and process is explained below.

Programs consist of sets of processes which communicate with each other via channels which provide statically defined, unidirectional, synchronized communication paths between pairs of processes. Processes communicate by reading or writing to named channels but only one process may write to a named channel and only one may read from it. On execution the operations of read and write on a channel are synchronized so that they occur simultaneously. Thus the input–output pair act as a distributed assignment with the variable named in the input process being assigned the value of the expression in the output process. Note that this is the only form of communication supported; shared variables are not allowed except for read only access.

2.2 THE LANGUAGE

Before considering the language in detail we should point out that occam is designed as a static language, that is, the storage requirements for both code and data have to be known at compile time. This imposes constraints on the language including the fact that various values have to be defined as constants.

2.2.1 Primitive processes

The basic unit of occam is the process, as stated above, which corresponds to a statement in a standard sequential programming language. The three primitive processes which form the basis of the occam language are:

1 the assignment process
variable := expression for example, x := 0
2 the input process
channel ? variable for example, ch1 ? a
3 the output process
channel ! expression for example, ch2 ! (b + 2)

Communication over a channel is synchronized so that an input operation can only occur when the corresponding output operation is ready and vice versa. Thus the combination of input and output operations provide for transmission of data between a pair of processes without buffering. If a pair of input–output processes are to be used for synchronization only, rather than the transmission of data, then the special syntax word ANY may be used in place of the variable and expression. As a shorthand, instead of writing multiple inputs or outputs on a channel as a sequence of input or output processes the items may be separated by semicolons using a single input or output. For example, the sequence:

```
ch ! 2
ch ! x
ch ! 3
```

could be written as:

```
ch ! 2;x;3
```

Two other primitive processes are included in the language. The null process, SKIP, caters for the cases where a process is required by the syntax but no action is required by the programmer. A further primitive process, STOP, is provided which starts, never proceeds and never terminates. This process is not used very often in programming but it is the natural action to specify if some unexpected error occurs.

2.2.2 Programming conventions

Like other programming languages, identifiers are comprised of a string of letters and digits of which the first must be a letter. Both upper and lower case letters are supported and we use the convention in this book of writing keywords such as STOP and SKIP, which are reserved words, in upper case and user defined names such as ‘x’ and ‘ch’ in lower case.

In occam comments may be written anywhere on a line. They begin with two minus signs and terminate with the end of line, for example:

```
ch ! x   -- send x along channel ch
-- this is a comment line on its own
```

Normally each process is defined on a single line. However, processes may be broken over several lines providing that the compiler can detect that the line has been broken. The places where a line may be split are difficult to define but splitting a line directly after an operator or separator, such as comma, usually works. Continuation lines must be indented at least as far as the first line.

2.2.3 Constructors

In the same way that statements can be combined into groups in a sequential language using constructors such as FOR and WHILE, so processes in occam can be combined into larger processes using constructors. The simplest form of process constructor is SEQ which implies that the following block of processes will be performed sequentially, that is, a process will not start until its predecessor has terminated. Another process constructor, PAR, specifies that the processes in the following block will be executed in parallel with each other, that is, conceptually all the processes start together and the PAR process does not terminate until all the constituent processes have terminated. Blocks in occam are represented by indentation in the program layout, rather than **begin . . . end** brackets as in other block structured languages. New blocks are indented two spaces more than the surrounding text. Note that this indentation is part of the syntax of occam and not just a feature to improve the layout of the program. For example, the code to set the variable x to 4 and the variable y to 6 could be:

```
SEQ
  x := 4
  y := 6
```

This specifies that the two assignments are performed in the order specified but since they are independent of one another they could be performed at the same time. This would be coded as:

```
PAR
  x := 4
  y := 6
```

In this case the textual ordering of the two assignment processes is irrelevant. Hierarchical nesting of blocks is allowed, provided that each block is indented by an extra two spaces. Thus:

```
PAR
  SEQ
    x := 4
    y := 3
  SEQ
    a := 1
    b := 2
    c := 3
```

specifies that the two sequences of assignments are to be executed in parallel.

As in sequential languages there are a number of other constructors, such as WHILE and IF available in occam. For example, a loop to initialize a vector x of integers of length n could be coded as:

```
SEQ
  j := 0
  WHILE j<n
    SEQ
      x[j] := 0
      j := j + 1
```

As this example shows vector subscripting starts at 0 in occam. The language also has an iterative construct, called a replicator, which may be combined with SEQ and PAR, which could reduce the code of the example above to:

```
SEQ j = [0 FOR n]
  x[j] := 0
```

which has the same effect as the code for a FOR loop in a standard sequential language except that the body of the replicated construct should be considered as being copied the requisite number of times rather than being in a loop. In other words,

```
SEQ j = [0 FOR 2]
  x[j] := 0
```

is shorthand notation for:

```
SEQ
  x[0] := 0
  x[1] := 0
```

Since, in this case, the assignments in the body are independent, PAR could be substituted for SEQ. However, it should be noted that in some implementations the number of parallel processes has to be known at compile-time hence both the base and the count of the replicator, 0 and n in one of the examples, would have to be constants if PAR was used. Notice that the starting value and count of the replicator are given, in this case 0 and n, respectively, and so the body is replicated over the vector elements from 0 to n−1.

The IF constructor is similar to the IF found in traditional sequential languages except that the syntax and layout are rather different. To illustrate this we give an example where an identifier 'x' is given the value 1,0 or −1 depending on whether the expression 'a + b' is positive, zero or negative.

```
IF
  (a + b) > 0
    x := 1
  (a + b) = 0
    x := 0
  (a + b) < 0
    x := -1
```

The conditions are evaluated in order and the first one which evaluates to true causes the following process to be executed. Note that conditions are indented from the IF and that at least one condition must be true when the IF is evaluated, otherwise an error will be signalled. The standard Boolean constants TRUE and FALSE are predefined in the language so the example above could equally well be coded as:

```
IF
  (a + b) > 0
    x := 1
  (a + b) = 0
    x := 0
  TRUE
    x := -1
```

since the final condition will only be evaluated if all the other conditions are false. Thus having TRUE as one of the conditions is equivalent to the **else** clause of a sequential **if** statement. The use of TRUE with the null process SKIP enables IF statements to be coded which would require no **else** clause in a sequential language, for example,

```
IF x<5 THEN y := y + 1;
```

in Pascal is equivalent to:

```
IF
  x<5
    y := y + 1
  TRUE
    SKIP
```

in occam. Replicators may be used with IF but their use is not very common.

A process constructor which does not have an analog in most sequential languages is the ALT construct. This construct is based on the concept of guarded commands first described by Dijkstra (Dijkstra, 1975). It acts as a non-deterministic select of one of a number of guarded processes. A guard consists of an input process or SKIP, or the conjunction of either of these simple guards with an expression, written as expression & simple guard, for example, (a>b) & in?x. On execution all of the guards are evaluated and *one* of the guarded processes, chosen non-deterministically and corresponding to a true guard, is executed. A true guard is one in which the input process has data waiting, the expression is true or one in which both of these conditions holds. If none of the guards evaluates to true, execution is delayed until at least one becomes true. The construct is frequently used so that a process may choose from one of a number of inputs. For example, if a process acts as a multiplexer, accepting input from more than one source, but not concurrently, and passing it on to another process it could be coded as:

```
WHILE TRUE
  ALT
    a?x
      z!x
    b?x
      z!x
    .
    .
    .
```

Notice that each guard is indented two spaces from the ALT and that each guarded process is indented a further two spaces. Here the guards are input processes which will only evaluate to true if the input can take place, that is, if the output process connected to the same channel is ready to output. The overall action of this example is to serialize possible concurrent input on different channels to the process and send output to channel z.

ALT may also take a replicator. For example, if the multiplexer example above had input channels a[0], a[1], etc. instead of a,b etc. then the code could have been written as:

```
ALT i=[0 FOR n]
  a[i] ? x
    z ! x
```

if there were *n* inputs to the multiplexer.

2.2.4 Named processes

In a similar manner to that in which a block of statements in a sequential language can be made into a named procedure so a block of processes in occam may be named and may have parameters. For example, a named process to initialize the components of a vector x of length n to zero could be:

```
PROC init(VAR x[],VALUE n)=
  SEQ j = [0 FOR n]
    x[j] := 0    :
```

The definition of the named process starts with PROC followed by the name of the process and a list of formal parameters in brackets, terminated with '='. Following the body of the code is a colon, the symbol which terminates all definitions in occam. Parameters to named processes may take one of three forms: VAR, which specifies call by address, VALUE, which specifies call by value and CHAN which specifies that the parameter is a channel name. As shown in this example the size of a vector parameter is not given explicitly, but the brackets are required to show that the parameter is a vector. Note that the body of a named process is indented. Named processes are instantiated by mentioning their name in another process; recursive processes are not allowed.

2.2.5 Data and data structures

In spite of the superficial similarity of its control structures to Pascal, occam is a low-level language and, like other low-level languages, few data types are supported and those which are depend on the underlying memory organization. Occam supports operations on words which are some implementation dependent multiple of 8-bit bytes. Vectors of words are supported, as we have seen previously, and vectors of bytes and channels are also allowed. Subscripting of all types of vectors starts at zero. Remembering that occam is a static language the size of the vectors must be known at compile time, that is, the size values used in the declaration must be constants.

Normally, variables, vectors, constants and channels have to be declared before they are used, although identifiers used as replicator counters do not. Channels and vectors of channels are defined in a CHAN declaration, for example,

```
CHAN a,c,g,d[5],king[67] :
```

Variables and vectors of variables are declared in a VAR declaration, for example,

```
VAR b,h[16],z[BYTE 20],x[n] :
```

This declares a variable b, a word vector h of size 16, a byte vector z of size 20 and a word vector x of size n. The variables created are undefined; variables cannot be initialized in a declaration. Note the colon terminating the definitions. Remember that vectors start from zero, hence the vector h is defined for h[0] to h[15]. In the above declaration it is assumed that n has been defined previously, for example, by a constant declaration such as:

```
DEF n = 10 :
```

It is also possible to declare vector constants:

```
DEF motor = TABLE [0,3,7,2] :
```

where the individual elements may be selected by the usual subscripting, for example, motor[1]. String constants may be defined also:

```
DEF str = "This is a string" :
```

Strings are stored as byte vectors with the count in byte 0, thus the code

```
SEQ i = [1 FOR str[BYTE 0]]
  out!str[BYTE i]
```

would output the characters of the stored string along the channel out. Note the use of the keyword BYTE when accessing a byte vector.

By default, numbers are assumed to be decimal; hexadecimal numbers may be used if preceded by a # sign.

Single characters may be represented by enclosing them in single quotes. Asterisk is used as an escape character and the special combinations '*C','*N' and '*S' represent the characters for carriage return, newline and space respectively.

2.2.6 Expressions

Expressions are formed, as in other programming languages, by a sequence of operands separated by operators. The operators available in occam include the monadic operators – and NOT and the following dyadic operators.

1 arithmetic

+	plus
–	minus
*	multiply
/	divide
\	remainder

2 logical

/\	bitwise and
\/	bitwise or
><	bitwise exclusive or
NOT	bit inversion
<<	left shift (up)
>>	right shift (down)

	(the second operand of the shift operators denotes the required shift)
3 comparison	
<	less than
>	greater than
<=	less than or equals
>=	greater than or equals
=	equals
<>	not equal to
AND	Boolean and
OR	Boolean or

As mentioned previously, the standard Boolean constants TRUE and FALSE are predefined. As in other programming languages brackets are used to specify the evaluation order in expressions. This is especially important in occam since all operators have the same priority and there is no 'left to right' evaluation rule and therefore expressions may be evaluated in any order. For example, the expression 2 + 3 * 4 has to be coded as 2 + (3 * 4) in occam if it is to have its normal mathematical interpretation. Also it should be noted that the AND and OR operations evaluate their operands in left to right order and that the second operand is not evaluated unless required, for example, in the case of the following expression:

```
i < 16 AND h[i] = 5
```

i < 16 is evaluated first and only if this is true will h[i] = 5 be evaluated. Thus the array will only be accessed if i is less than 16 giving a mechanism for avoiding array access errors.

2.2.7 Input–output

External input and output are not defined as part of the occam language. Input–output devices are connected to occam programs by means of special channels which have to be defined by means of a channel declaration at the beginning of the program. The channel declaration takes the form:

```
CHAN identifier AT expression :
```

The peripheral acts as a process which performs either input or output over the named channel. A visual display unit acts as two devices; a keyboard device and a screen device. Thus the screen and keyboard of a terminal can be directly accessed by occam processes. Remembering that a channel may only be used by two processes, one to read and the other to write, use of devices by more than one occam process is prohibited. If multiple access is required then a multiplexer or demultiplexer process is required to interface the readers or writers to the devices as shown in the following examples. Standard operating system procedures on the computer on which the occam system is mounted usually allow screen output to be redirected to a printer to produce hard copy output. In addition to simple terminal input–output many implementations provide methods of reading and writing to files; the reader is referred to the manual for his particular implementation.

Input and output from external devices to occam, as can be seen from the description above, is very basic and similar to that provided in a typical assembly language. Thus the inputting and outputting of integers, for example, is tedious and involves converting from external to internal representation or vice versa. Anyone who programs regularly in occam soon develops a suite of named processes to do the required conversions on input and output.

2.2.8 Extra features

The language also includes a number of other features, such as slices which allow the programmer the ability to manipulate a set of vector elements together, but these features are not used in the examples in this book.

As well as the features described so far the language also includes a number of constructs to allow the user to specify how the set of occam processes is to be mapped on to a set of transputers. These are known as configuration features. A few of these features are discussed in Chapter 10 on real time applications, but the interested reader is referred to the occam manual for information on these extra features.

2.3 STRUCTURE OF AN occam PROGRAM

Having seen the basic constructs and data types of occam the question arises of how to put all this together to form a program. An occam program is simply a **process**; a possibly null set of declarations of constants, channels, variables and named processes followed by executable code. The executable code may be a single primitive process or it may be constructed from a set of primitive processes.

To illustrate this let us take a very simple program, one which inputs a character from the keyboard and echoes it on the screen of a VDU. This could be coded as

```
CHAN keyboard AT ... : -- implementation dependent value
CHAN screen AT ... : -- implementation dependent value
VAR x :
WHILE TRUE
  SEQ
    keyboard ? x
    screen ! x
```

Note that the definitions and the executable code are at the same level of indentation. The declaration of the keyboard and screen channels define the input and output channels to the VDU. The variable declaration declares x which is in scope for all the executable code which follows. This executable code is simply an infinite loop which continuously reads a character from the keyboard and echoes it on the screen without any formatting.

Remembering that a constructed process is simply a constructor and a number of primitive processes, each of which may be preceded by declarations, it is possible to rewrite this example as:

```
CHAN keyboard AT ... : -- implementation dependent value
CHAN screen AT ... : -- implementation dependent value
WHILE TRUE
  VAR x :
  SEQ
    keyboard ? x
    screen ! x
```

Here the scope of the variable x has been restricted to the sequence of input and output processes rather than to the whole WHILE process. It is good programming practice to restrict the scope of variables to the minimum so that the compiler can check for scoping errors. In the above example the channel declarations for keyboard and screen could have been moved with the variable declaration since the scope required is the same but conventionally all external channel declarations are placed at the beginning of the program.

Another possible coding for this example in terms of a named process is:

```
CHAN keyboard AT ... : -- implementation dependent value
CHAN screen AT ... : -- implementation dependent value
PROC echo =
  WHILE TRUE
    VAR x :
    SEQ
      keyboard ? x
      screen ! x :

echo
```

This program consists of two channel declarations, a named process declaration and the executable code which is the instantiation of the named process. Note that, as subprogram instantiation in Pascal, process instantiation does not require empty brackets for processes with no parameters.

Having shown how to write a simple program involving input and output to a VDU the reader should be able to convert any simple high-level language program into the equivalent occam program, for example, a program to sort a set of numbers or to generate factorials. This, however, is not the purpose of occam. The reason for using occam is to use the natural concurrency in the problem to produce a solution which uses multiple processes. To do this requires a different way of thinking and this is often quite difficult for the programmer brought up to think sequentially. We will illustrate what we mean by a simple example. Consider the case of searching a set of characters for a particular one. One obvious coding, ignoring the input of the required character and the output of the result, would be as shown in Fig. 2.1.

```
notendloop := TRUE   -- initially keep going round loop
WHILE notendloop
  IF
    ch = store[i]   -- is it value required?
      SEQ
        result := TRUE      -- if so report this
        notendloop := FALSE   -- and exit loop
    TRUE
      SEQ
        i := i+1   -- increment store pointer
        IF
          i > n   -- is it end of stored values?
            SEQ
              result := FALSE   -- if so report not there
              notendloop := FALSE   -- and terminate loop
          TRUE
            SKIP
```

Fig. 2.1 Simple search program.

This is the occam equivalent of the standard sequential method of searching. However there is inherent parallelism in this process since each of the store values could be compared with ch at the same time in just the same way in which the comparison would be done in an associative memory. To do this we would need a set of processes each of which stores one of the values and which compares this value with any input, generating true or false depending on the result of the comparison. A further process is required to collect the results of the comparison and generate the overall result. This solution can be expressed as shown in Fig. 2.2.

```
DEF n = ... : -- number of values is a constant
CHAN answer[n] -- channels to communicate reply to proc
PAR
  PAR i = [0 FOR n] -- set of processes to do comparison
    VAR store[i] :  -- value for each process
    IF
      store[i] = ch
        answer[i]!TRUE
      TRUE
        answer[i]!FALSE
  VAR result,i :  -- collection process
  SEQ
    result := FALSE
    notendofloop := TRUE
    i := 0
    WHILE notendofloop -- cycle around results
      VAR bool :
      SEQ
        answer[i]?bool
        IF
          bool = TRUE -- stop when one positive reply
            SEQ
              result := TRUE
              notendofloop := FALSE
          TRUE
            IF
              i = n - 1
                notendofloop := FALSE
              TRUE
                i := i+1
```

Fig. 2.2 Parallel search program.

There are a number of points about this solution. Firstly, although this solution contains some apparent parallelism, the PAR constructor is used in the code, there is no guarantee that this solution will produce an answer faster than the previous solution; an analysis of the algorithm is required to answer this question. Some pitfalls which could occur are that the parallel algorithm involves as many steps as the sequential one, at least for some patterns of input data, and that apparent parallelism in the solution is not real because synchronization between the parallel processes implies that some processes have to be executed before others. Less apparent problems include a consideration of the overheads of implementing the parallelism and synchronization which could, in some cases, outweigh any real parallelism. These details cannot be discovered for any particular solution without a detailed analysis of the algorithms. Secondly, the solution presented here exhibits a problem which is common to many solutions which use parallelism. In order to make the solution more efficient the collection process terminates as soon as it has discovered a positive result. The result of this is that a number of the search processes become deadlocked, that is, blocked forever trying to output, because the collection process has terminated and will not take part in communication. Program termination is therefore untidy with several processes being deadlocked rather than being terminated. The solution to this in this case is for the collection process to report its result as soon as possible but to continue to communicate with all the search processes until all the replies have been received so that all the processes terminate normally (see Fig. 2.3).

```
DEF n = ... : -- number of values is a constant
CHAN answer[n] -- channels to communicate reply to proc
PAR
  PAR i = [0 FOR n] -- set of search processes
    VAR store[i] :  -- value for each process
    IF
      store[i] = ch
        answer[i]!TRUE
      TRUE
        answer[i]!FALSE
  VAR result,i :  -- collection process
  SEQ
    result := FALSE
    i := 0
    WHILE i<>n -- cycle around results
      VAR bool :
      SEQ
        answer[i]?bool
        IF
          bool = TRUE -- stop when one positive reply
            SEQ
              result := TRUE
              -- communicate or print result
          TRUE
            i := i+1
```

Fig. 2.3 Parallel search program with termination.

The termination problem is one which will occur again in this book and is one which is sometimes difficult to solve in a neat fashion.

This example has illustrated some of the major problems of concurrent programming; the need for a different approach to problem solution, the pitfalls of apparent parallelism and the problems of termination and deadlock.

2.4 EXAMPLES

We now give two larger examples of occam programs to illustrate some more of the features of language.

2.4.1 Modelling of an AND gate

Firstly consider modelling of a hardware component, an AND gate (see Fig. 2.4).

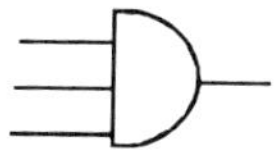

Fig. 2.4 3 input AND gate.

An occam process to model such a gate is given in Fig. 2.5.

```
-- and process
--
PROC andgate(VALUE n,CHAN in[],out)=
--
-- modelling n input AND gate
--
  VAR inp[10] :          -- note array bound must be a constant
  SEQ                        -- or a symbol defined as a constant
    SEQ i=[0 FOR n]          -- input places initialled
      inp[i]:=0
    WHILE TRUE
      VAR temp :
      SEQ
        temp:=1
        SEQ j=[0 FOR n]
          temp:=temp/\inp[j] -- calc new output
        out!temp             -- and send out
        ALT i=[0 FOR n]
          in[i]?inp[i]       -- wait for new input
            SKIP         :
```

Fig. 2.5 occam process to model an AND gate.

The wires are modelled by channels and the number of inputs is a parameter to the process. Initially the input places, inp, are set to zero and the output calculated. The process then waits in the ALT construct for input from another process over one of the input channels. The process calculates the new output arising from this new input, outputs it and waits again in the ALT construct for more input. To test this process we need to produce an occam program which corresponds to Fig. 2.6.

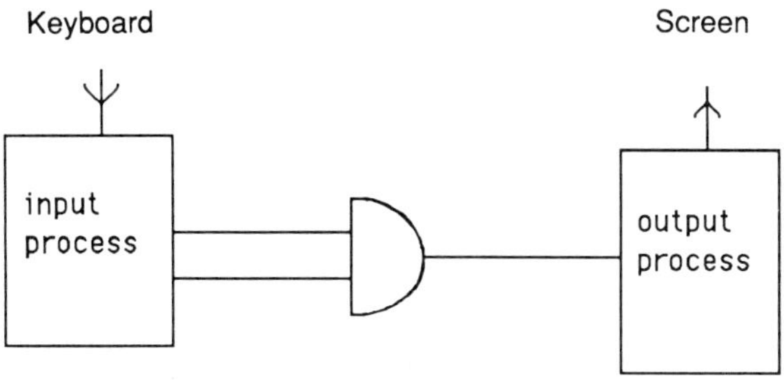

Fig. 2.6 Testing an AND gate.

Using the input–output conventions of the Inmos VAX OPS occam system this can be coded as shown in Fig. 2.7.

```
DEF Endbuffer = -3 :     -- token to flush buffers
CHAN Screen at 1:        -- channel to screen
CHAN Keyboard at 2:      -- channel to keyboard

PROC andgate(VALUE n,CHAN in[],out)=
        .
  body of and as above
        .
          :

PROC input(CHAN out1,out2)=
  WHILE TRUE
    VAR char :
    SEQ
      Keyboard?char       -- get char from keyboard
      Screen!char         -- echo it
      Screen!Endbuffer    -- flush screen buffer
      out1!(char-'0')     -- convert to integer
      Keyboard?char
      Screen!char
      Screen!Endbuffer
      out2!(char-'0')     :

Proc output(CHAN out)=
  WHILE TRUE
    VAR char :
    SEQ
      out?char            -- get char to output
      Screen!(char+'0')   -- send ASCII code to screen
      Screen!Endbuffer    :

CHAN i[2],o   :       -- defining channels between processes
PAR                   -- all processes running in parallel
  andgate(2,i,o)
  input(i[0],i[1])
  output(o)
```

Fig. 2.7 occam progam to test the model of an AND gate.

There is one problem with this solution: it disobeys the rules of occam! The Screen channel is used by two different processes for output which is illegal use of a channel. Although this program will work on most the occam implementations that we know of, the correct solution is to add a multiplexer to which all screen output is sent. The code in Fig. 2.8 shows this amended solution.

2.4.2 Shortest path in a directed graph

As the final example in this chapter consider the problem of finding the shortest path in a directed graph. We simplify the problem by making all the edges of length one, thus making the shortest path equivalent to traversal of the least number of edges (see Fig. 2.9).

```
CHAN Screen at 1:          -- channel to screen
CHAN Keyboard at 2:        -- channel to keyboard
DEF Endbuffer = -3 :       -- token to flush buffers

PROC andgate(VALUE n,CHAN in[],out)=
          .
  body of and as above
          .
              :

PROC input(CHAN out1,out2,out3)=
  WHILE TRUE
    VAR char :
    SEQ
      Keyboard?char         -- get char from keyboard
      out3!char             -- send char to mpxr for screen
      out1!(char-'0')       -- convert to integer
      Keyboard?char
      out3!char
      out2!(char-'0')     :

PROC output(CHAN out,out1)=
  WHILE TRUE
    VAR char :
    SEQ
      out?char
      out1!(char+'0')     :  -- send output to mpxr

PROC multiplexer(CHAN in1,in2,out)=
  WHILE TRUE
    VAR val  :
    ALT                       -- serialise output to Screen
      in1?val
        SEQ
          out!val
          out!Endbuffer
      in2?val
        SEQ
          out!val
          out!Endbuffer   :

CHAN i[2],o,mpxr1,mpxr2   :
PAR                     -- all processes running in parallel
  andgate(2,i,o)
  input(i[0],i[1],mpxr1)
  output(o,mpxr2)
  multiplexer(mpxr1,mpxr2,Screen)
```

Fig. 2.8 Modified testing program with screen multiplexer.

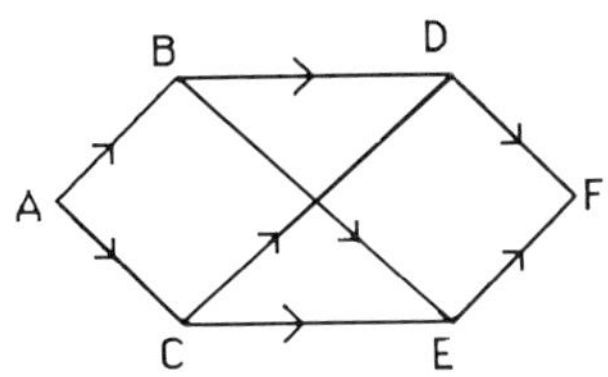

Fig. 2.9 A directed graph.

If we model the edges as channels and the nodes as processes, we have three different types of process; the origin process, A in Fig. 2.9, the destination process, F in the graph above, and the internal processes. One possible solution is for the origin process to send out a message with the path length to the receiving nodes along all its output channels. In our simplified problem all the path lengths are unity. The internal processes receive messages and, if the path length quoted in the message is smaller than any they have received before, broadcast that message along their output channels, after incrementing the path length to the receiving node. Eventually messages reach the destination node which stores the smallest path length it receives. One problem is that the destination node does not know when it has received its last message and therefore when it has the minimum path length. To signal this a set of terminator tokens can be broadcast through the network and when these have all reached the destination node then the current value stored is the shortest route (see Fig. 2.10).

```
DEF maxval=20,termin=99  :

PROC originnode(VALUE m,CHAN out[])=
-- outputs path length to internal nodes
-- and then terminator tokens
  SEQ
    SEQ i=[0 FOR m]
      out[i]!1
    SEQ i=[0 FOR m]
      out[i]!termin   :

PROC internalnode(VALUE n,m,CHAN in[],out[])=
-- stores minimum input path length on any input
-- broadcasts any received value
-- less than the current minimum
-- broadcasts terminator token after
-- receipt of same from all input channels
  VAR minval,endcount  :
  SEQ
    minval:=maxval            -- initially 'infinity'
    endcount:=0
    WHILE TRUE
      VAR val :
      ALT i=[0 FOR n]
        in[i]?val             -- accept any input
          IF
            val=termin
              IF
                endcount=n-1    -- all termin recd
                  SEQ i=[0 FOR n]
                    out[i]!termin   -- broadcast termin
                TRUE
                  endcount:=endcount+1
            val<minval
              PAR
                minval:=val
                SEQ i=[0 FOR m]
                  out[i]!(val+1)-- broadcast minval
            TRUE
              SKIP   :
```

```
PROC destinationnode(VALUE n,CHAN in[],numberout)=
-- stores the minimum value input and
-- outputs this minimum when all terminators received
  VAR mindist  :
  SEQ
    mindist:=maxval         -- initially 'infinity'
    WHILE TRUE
      VAR val :
      ALT i=[0 FOR n]
        in[i]?val           -- accept any input
          IF
            val=termin
              IF
                endcount=n-1  -- all termin recd
                  SEQ
                    numberout!mindist  -- output min
                    STOP               -- and stop
                TRUE
                  IF
                    val<mindist
                      mindist:=val
                    TRUE
                      SKIP   :

PROC arc(CHAN in,out)=
  WHILE TRUE
    VAR val  :
    SEQ
      in?val
      out!val   :

CHAN aout[2],bin[1],bout[2],cin[1],cout[2],din[2],
     dout[1],ein[2],eout[1],fin[2],screenout  :
PAR
  originnode(2,aout)            -- set up nodes
  internalnode(1,2,bin,bout)
  internalnode(1,2,cin,cout)
  internalnode(2,1,din,dout)
  internalnode(2,1,ein,eout)
  destinationnode(2,fin,screenout)  -- not Screenout
  arc(aout[0],cin[0])           -- set up arcs
  arc(aout[1],bin[0])
  arc(bout[0],din[0])
  arc(bout[1],ein[0])
  arc(cout[0],din[1])
  arc(cout[1],ein[1])
  arc(dout[0],fin[0])
  arc(eout[0],fin[1])

-- plus module to print contents of screenout channel
```

Fig. 2.10   occam program to find the shortest path in a directed graph.

This solution may look peculiar since we have introduced eight arc processes in our solution. The reason for this is due to a naming problem in occam. The only way to make a general purpose node process is to make the parameters vectors since a variable number of parameters is not allowed. By doing this a naming problem arises since output and input names do not match. One solution, the one adopted here, is to insert buffers in the arcs simply to rename them.

SUMMARY Chapter 2

The basic constructs of the occam language, a low-level language intended for programming transputers, have been presented in this chapter. The static model of computation on which the language is based consists of a set of processes which communicate with each other via named, synchronous, unidirectional channels. The basic elements of the language are a set of primitive processes, including assignment, input, output, SKIP and STOP, and a set of constructors, including SEQ, PAR, WHILE, IF and ALT, which allow more complex processes to be constructed.

The major difference between occam and a standard programming language such as Pascal is the inclusion of the PAR constructor in occam. This allows the programmer to express parallelism in program code and thus allows him to produce problem solutions which can be directly executed on an interconnected set of transputers.

EXERCISES Chapter 2

E2.1 There is a neater way of coding the sequential searching algorithm than that given in this chapter which uses nested IF's. Can you discover this coding?

E2.2 Modify the program given for modelling an AND gate to model OR and NOT gates also.

E2.3 Modify the network program given above to output the route of the shortest path as well as the shortest distance.

E2.4 Modify the network program to increase the amount of concurrency in the solution. Can you do much better than the solution outlined in Fig. 2.10?

E2.5 A well-known problem in computing is the Firing Line problem. In this problem a set of processes are connected in a line, that is, each, apart from the end processes, is connected to its two nearest neighbours. One of the processes at the end of the line has a button attached to it and each process can control a light. The problem is to get each process to turn on its light at the same time some time after the button has been pressed. The number of processes in the line should not be explicitly coded into any process. Write an occam program to solve this problem, assuming that the button input and light outputs are made available via channels of these names.

3

THE BASIC COMMUNICATION MECHANISMS

The model of a concurrent system implicit in occam is a set of concurrent processes which communicate synchronously via named channels. This is one model of communication but there are many more and in this chapter we explore many of the possible unidirectional communication models, modelled in occam.

3.1 COMMUNICATION MECHANISMS

There are a number of 'standard' ways of communicating between processes and in this next section we show how some of these can be simulated in occam. The simulation is useful in that it gives some insight into these basic communication mechanisms and the examples themselves act as illustrations of the good and bad points of the occam language. In this chapter we assume only a single reader and a single writer process; a condition which is relaxed in the next chapter. In our examples we use a procedural interface to each process to hide the details of the protocol requirements.

3.1.1 Example 1 – shared variable

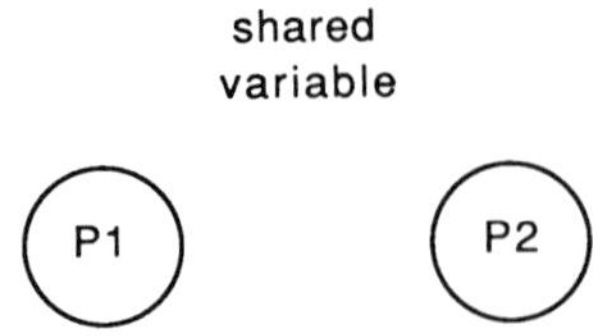

Fig. 3.1 Shared variable model.

One of the simplest forms of communication between processes is seemingly the use of **global** (or **shared**) variables (see Fig. 3.2).

```
VAR b :                -- shared variable

-- interface protocols

PROC write (VALUE v ) =
  b := v   :

PROC read ( VAR v ) =
  v := b   :

-- client processes

PAR
  VAR x :
  ....write(x)....

  VAR y :
  ....read(y)....
```

Fig. 3.2 occam code for shared variable.

This solution is, however, illegal occam code, since the write process assigns a value to the variable b and the rules of occam specifically exclude this use of a shared variable; shared variables may only be read. The reason for this is that situations which are unsafe could occur, for example, if two processes which wrote to a shared variable occurred inside a PAR construct then the final value of the variable would depend on the timing of the execution of the two processes. In the worst case the value of the variable could be a mixture of the two values written because of interference. To obtain a safe solution to the use of shared variables by concurrent processes we need to encapsulate the shared variable into a process which enforces the correct synchronization constraints.

3.1.2 Example 2 – encapsulated shared variable

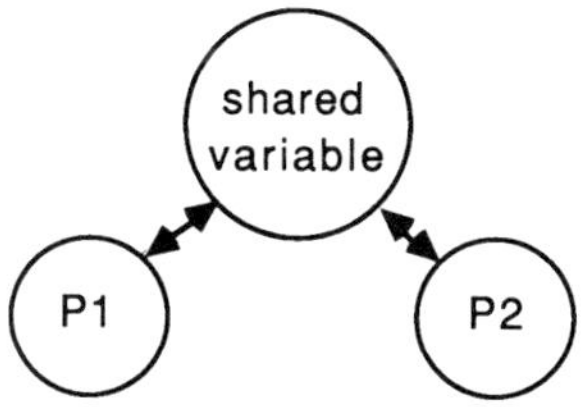

Fig. 3.3 Encapsulated shared variable model.

The synchronization constraints for access to any global variable are that writers may only update the value in mutual exclusion with other writers and readers, but any number of readers may be active concurrently; the standard readers'–writers' problem (Courtois *et al.*, 1971). In order to maintain this synchronization discipline in concurrent systems the global variable must be encapsulated into a process, as shown in Fig. 3.4.

```
CHAN w,r,p:
PAR
  -- encapsulated global variable
  VAR b:
  SEQ
    w?b            -- need a write to initialise variable
    WHILE TRUE
      ALT       -- accept reads and writes in any seq
        w?b
          SKIP
        p?ANY   -- accept read request
          r!b   -- send value to be read

  -- interface protocols

  PROC write(VALUE v)=
    w!v  :

  PROC read(VAR v)=
    SEQ
      p!ANY     -- request global value
      r?v  :    -- read global value

  -- client processes

  PAR
    VAR x :
    ....write(x)....

    VAR y :
    ....read(y)....
```

Fig. 3.4 occam code for encapsulated shared variable.

Here we see one of the asymmetries of occam; outputs may not appear in guards. To program around this restriction, the read process has to request the encapsulation process to send the shared value instead of just reading it.

This solution allows serialized (sequential) access to the variable. It thus allows any sequence of read and write operations on the shared variable after an initial write, but not concurrent access.

3.1.3 Example 3 – synchronized communication

Fig. 3.5 Synchronized communication model.

Processes do not have to communicate indirectly via shared variables; they can communicate directly. However, if they are to communicate directly they must synchronize their actions of reading and writing. Processes in occam can communicate directly via the use of a channel which ensures the necessary synchronization. This is equivalent to distributed assignment, in this case y := x (see Fig. 3.6).

```
CHAN c :

-- interface protocols

PROC put ( VALUE v ) =
  c!v   :

PROC get ( VAR v ) =
  c?v   :

-- client processes

PAR
  VAR x :
  ....put(x)...

  VAR y :
  ....get(y)....
```

Fig. 3.6 occam code for synchronized communication.

3.1.4 Example 4 – single slot buffer

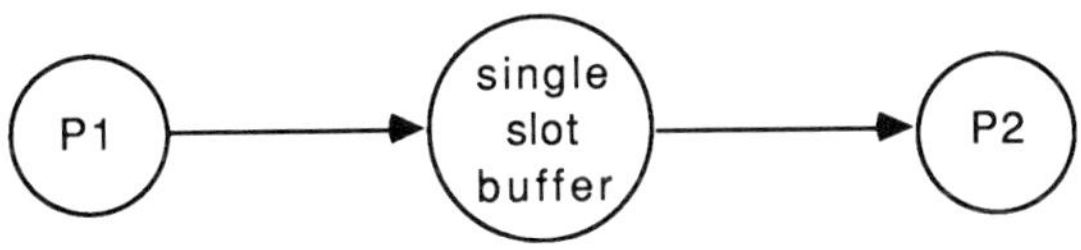

Fig. 3.7 Single slot buffer model.

Another means of communication is via a **buffer**. This decouples the reader and writer allowing the processes to operate asynchronously. The implication is that the processes can execute at their own speed but this is only true if the buffer is empty. If the buffer is full then the sender must wait until the receiver reads the previous value; that is, the rate of progress of the sender and receiver are linked. The synchronization requirements, for a single buffer, are for a write operation to be followed by a read operation, cyclically. The simplest type of buffer contains a single slot (see Fig. 3.8).

```
CHAN w,r :
PAR

  -- communication buffer

  WHILE TRUE
    VAR b :      -- single slot buffer
    SEQ
      w?b      -- accept a write operation
      r!b      -- accept a read operation

  -- interface protocols

  PROC put(VALUE v)=
    w!v :

  PROC get(VAR v)=
    r?v :

  -- client processes (decoupled by 1)

  PAR
    VAR x :
    ....put(x)....

    VAR y :
    ....get(y)....
```

Fig. 3.8 occam code for single slot buffer.

Because we know the ordering requirements of buffer access, put followed by get cyclically, we do not require the request – receive protocol, as used in the case of an encapsulated global variable, to perform the get operation.

3.1.5 Example 5 – multi-slot buffer

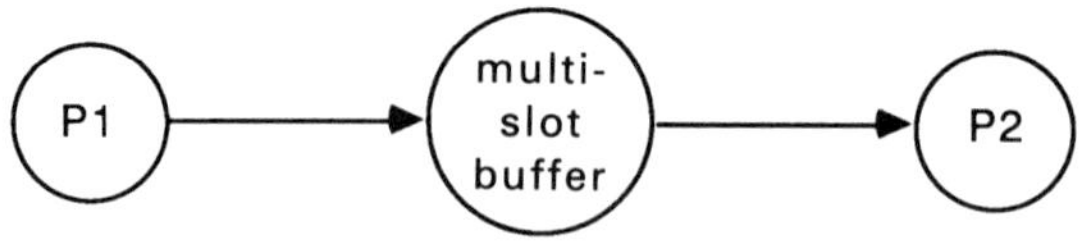

Fig. 3.9 Multi-slot buffer model.

The single slot buffer can be generalized to a **multi-slot buffer**, or **queue**, (Dijkstra, 1965) where readers and writers access different ends of the buffer or queue and may access concurrently provided that the conditions of buffer overflow and buffer underflow are not violated (see Fig. 3.10).

Notice that we allow concurrency and hence we do not know the

```
DEF d=... :        -- set to the no. of slots in the buffer
CHAN w,r,p :
PAR

  -- communications buffer

  VAR h,t,k : -- head pointer,tail pointer
              -- and count of number in buffer
  SEQ
    h:=0  -- initially nothing in buffer
    t:=0
    k:=0
    WHILE TRUE
      VAR b[d] : -- buffer
      ALT -- accept put and get in any order subject to
        k<d & w?b[t] -- write slot avail. and write req
          SEQ
            t:=(t+1)\d  -- update tail pointer
            k:=k+1      -- update no. in buffer
        k>0 & p?ANY   -- read slot avail. and read req.
          SEQ
            r!b[h]      -- send buffer value
            h:=(h+1)\d  -- update head pointer
            k:=k-1      -- update no. in buffer

  -- interface protocols

  PROC put(VALUE v)=
    w!v :

  PROC get(VAR v)=
    SEQ
      p!ANY
      r?v :

  -- client processes (decoupled by d)

  PAR
    VAR x :
    ....put(x)....

    VAR y :
    ....get(y)....
```

Fig. 3.10 occam code for multi-slot buffer.

ordering of read and write operations so we do need the request–receive protocol for read operations here. In this solution we have to check for buffer underflow and overflow as well as buffering the values because we do not know the ordering of requests and we do not wish to restrict them.

3.1.6 Example 6 – signal

Fig. 3.11 Control signal model.

Processes often only wish to synchronize with one another rather than to communicate data. This is referred to as a signal. It may be simulated over an occam channel by the use of the ANY construct (see Fig. 3.12).

```
CHAN c :

-- client processes

PAR
  ....c!ANY....

  ....c?ANY....
```

Fig. 3.12 occam code for a control model.

In this example the two processes communicate over the channel c and are therefore synchronized but the data sent over the channel, represented by ANY, corresponds to any bit pattern and is discarded by the receiver.

3.1.7 Example 7 – binary semaphore

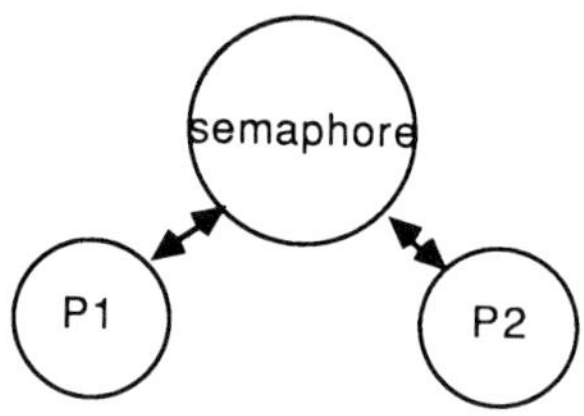

Fig. 3.13 Binary semaphore model.

A common requirement amongst co-operating processes is for access to resources to be mutually exclusive. This can be achieved using a binary semaphore (Dijkstra, 1965), as shown in Fig. 3.14.

The channels p and v act as a **semaphore**; a binary semaphore in this case. The semaphore process only accepts requests along the p and v channels cyclically in that order. Thus processes requesting use of the p and v channel in sequence will execute in mutual exclusion. Note the similarity between this solution and that of the single slot buffer. This solution is illegal in occam since both client processes share the channels p and v. A legal solution is given in the next chapter.

```
CHAN p,v :  -- channels to request P and V operations
PAR

  -- semaphore process

  WHILE TRUE
    SEQ
      p?ANY  -- allow P and V operations in sequence
      v?ANY

  -- interface protocols

  PROC acq =
    p!ANY :  -- acquire operation is P

  PROC rel =
    v!ANY :  -- release operation is Q

  -- client processes

  PAR
    SEQ
      ....acq....rel....

    SEQ
      ....acq....rel....
```

Fig. 3.14 occam code for a binary semaphore.

3.1.8 Example 8 – general semaphore

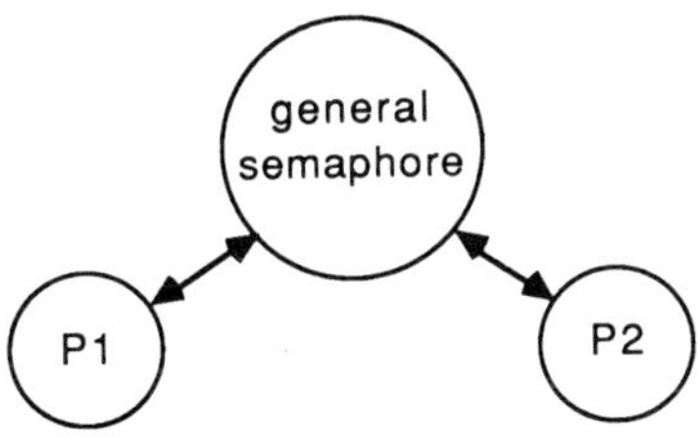

Fig. 3.15 General semaphore model.

General semaphores, which can take values other than 0 and 1, are often required as well as binary ones. They can be modelled in occam as shown in Fig. 3.16.

This solution allows for a number of resources to be acquired and released, albeit one at a time. Perhaps not surprisingly, this solution is very similar to the multi-slot buffer. It is illegal in occam for the same reason as the binary semaphore.

```
DEF nclient = ... :  -- set to no. of clients
DEF d = ? : -- max value of semaphore
CHAN p,v :  -- channels for P and V operations
PAR

  -- semaphore process

  VAR k :  -- keeps count of semaphore value
  SEQ
    k := 0
    WHILE TRUE
      ALT
        k<d & p?ANY     -- req to acq and req allowed
          k := k + 1
        k>0 & v?ANY     -- req to rel and req allowed
          k := k - 1

  -- interface protocols

  PROC acq =
    p!ANY   :

  PROC rel =
    v!ANY   :

  -- client processes

  PAR i = [0 FOR nclient]
    SEQ
      ....acq..acq..acq..rel..rel..rel...
```

Fig. 3.16 occam code for a general semaphore.

3.1.9 Example 9 – multi-slot buffer with separate index processes

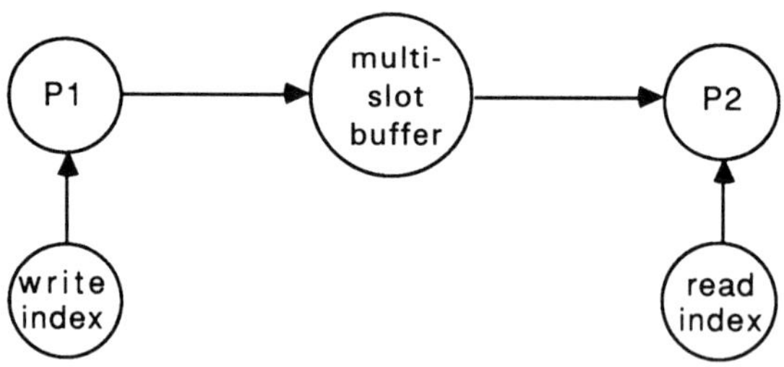

Fig. 3.17 Multi-slot buffer model with index processes.

Returning to the multi-slot buffer of Example 5, a different solution with more concurrency can be obtained if it is assumed that the act of gaining a buffer slot index is divorced from reading or writing to that slot. Using this indexing technique there are two possible solutions to the buffer. Firstly, the buffer can be regarded as a d-slot buffer with the encapsulation processes giving permission to obtain an index into the buffer to read and write (see Fig. 3.18).

```
DEF d=... : -- set to number of slots in the buffer
CHAN pw,vw,pr,vr,xr,xw :  -- permission to read and
                        -- terminated reading,permission
                        -- to write and terminated writing,
                        -- read index and write index

-- communication access

VAR b[d] :  -- d slot buffer
PAR
  PAR
    VAR k :  -- count of no. in buffer
    SEQ
      k:=0
      WHILE TRUE
        ALT
          k<d & pw?ANY -- req to write and slot empty
            SKIP
          vw?ANY       -- req to terminate writing
            k:=k+1
          k>0 & pr?ANY -- req to read and slot full
            SKIP
          vr?ANY       -- req to terminate reading
            k:=k-1
    -- write index
    VAR t :
    SEQ
      t:=0
      WHILE TRUE
        SEQ
          xw!t    -- send next write index to use
          t:=(t+1)\d  -- increment index
    --read index
    VAR h :
    SEQ
      h:=0
      WHILE TRUE
        SEQ
          xr!h    -- send next read index to use
          h:=(h+1)\d  -- increment index

  --interface protocols

  PROC put(VALUE v)=
    VAR i :
    SEQ
      pw!ANY      -- permission to write
      xw?i        -- obtain slot index
      b[i]:=v     -- put value into buffer
      vw!ANY :    -- signal end of write

  PROC get(VAR v)=
    VAR i :
     SEQ
       pr!ANY      -- permission to read
       xr?i        -- obtain slot index
       v:=b[i]     -- get value from buffer
       vr!ANY :    -- signal end of read

   -- client processes

   PAR
     VAR x :
     ....put(x)....

     VAR y :
     ....get(y)....
```

Fig. 3.18 occam code for multi-slot buffer with index processes.

This solution is strictly illegal occam since the global buffer b is both read and written by processes which are components of a parallel construct and therefore may be active concurrently. We give a legal solution in the next chapter.

This solution allows more concurrency than the one given in Example 5 since the read and write index code are separate processes and may be accessed concurrently with permission to obtain a slot and reading and writing the buffer slot. This gain in concurrency cannot be exploited with a single reader and writer.

3.1.10 Example 10 – multi-slot buffer as an array of single slots

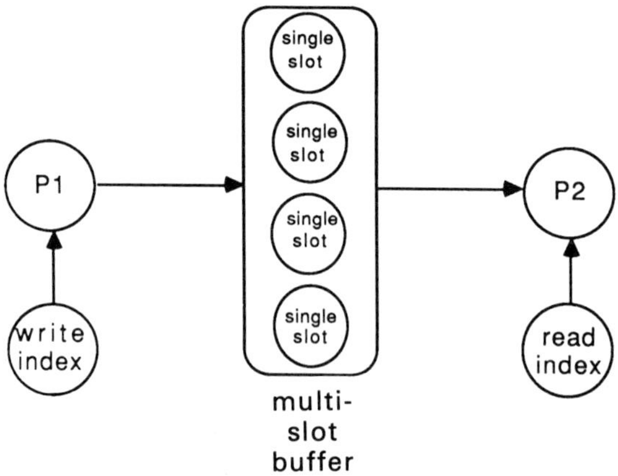

Fig. 3.19 Multi-slot buffer model with separate slots.

A different method of solving the multi-slot buffer problem is to assume the buffer is an array of single slot buffers. The problem of read/write synchronization is then dealt with by the individual buffers. We still need the separate index processes to index into the array of single slot buffers (see Fig. 3.20).

There are some differences between the solutions to the multi-slot buffer as given in Examples 9 and 10. In the former case access to the index processes and the buffer is controlled by the single semaphore whose count is kept in k. Thus processes are not allowed access to either the index process or the buffer until the appropriate slot in the buffer is full or empty, depending on whether the access is for reading or writing. In the case of Example 10 access to the index processes and the buffers is controlled separately and access to the index processes is unconstrained. Thus more concurrency is allowed in the latter case. With this extra concurrency comes some loss of ordering; we cannot assume that

```
DEF d=... : -- set to the number of slots in the buffer
CHAN w[d],r[d],xw,xr :  -- write channels,read channels
                        -- write index and read index channels
PAR

  -- array of single slot buffer processes

  PAR
    PAR i=[0 FOR d]
      WHILE TRUE
        VAR b :  -- buffer
        SEQ
          w[i]?b  -- write followed by
          r[i]!b  -- read cyclically
    -- write index
    VAR t :  -- write index counter
    SEQ
      t:=0
      WHILE TRUE
        xw!t    -- send write index
        t:=(t+1)\d
    -- read index
    VAR h :  -- read index counter
    SEQ
      h:=0
      WHILE TRUE
        xr!h    -- send read index
        h:=(h+1)\d

  -- interface protocols

  PROC put(VALUE v)=
    VAR i :
    SEQ
      xw?i        -- get index
      w[i]!v :    -- write value

  PROC get(VAR v)=
    VAR i :
    SEQ
      xr?i        -- get index
      r[i]?v :    -- read value

  -- client processes

  PAR
    VAR x :
    ....put(x)....

    VAR y :
    ....get(y)....
```

Fig. 3.20 occam code for multi-slot buffer with separate slots.

processes will access the buffer in the same order as they access the index processes, thus overtaking may occur. Whether the gain in concurrency in Example 10 is worthwhile or whether the consequent loss of ordering of access is important depends solely on the context in which the code is to be used. As in Example 9 we cannot make use of the extra concurrency in a single reader and single writer environment. We return to the discussion in the case of multiple readers and writers in the next chapter.

3.1.11 Example 11 – pipelined buffer

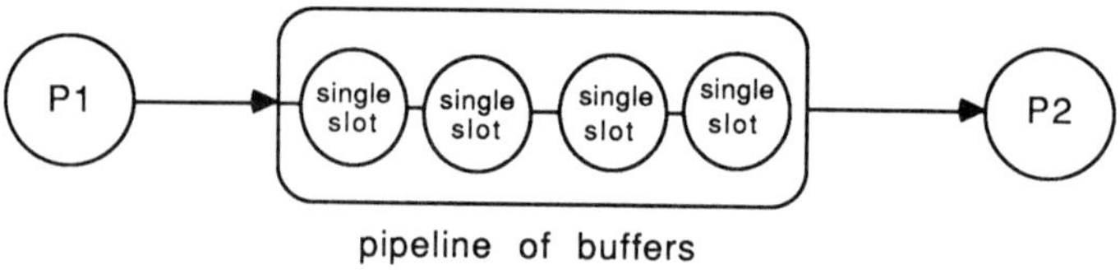

Fig. 3.21 Pipelined buffer model.

There is an alternative way to implement a multi-slot buffer and that is by means of a pipeline of buffer processes. Data to be buffered is inserted into the pipeline and the individual buffer processes ensure that data is always available at the head of the pipeline by moving it from the body to the head as soon as possible. The pipeline solution in occam is as shown in Fig. 3.22.

3.2 COMMUNICATION SCHEMES

In this chapter we have seen a number of different ways in which processes may communicate with each other. There are several ways in which they may be classified. Firstly, they may be classified into direct and indirect communication. The latter type require buffers in the communication path, whereas the former do not. In direct communication the producer and consumer have to be in synchronism at the point of data transfer and this is provided by the standard channel communication mechanism in occam. In the buffered case the producer and consumer can proceed at their own rate provided that the buffer is not full. Within the buffering schemes there is the possibility of introducing lower grain parallelism by only locking access to certain parts of the buffer rather than the complete buffer when data transfer is taking place. Whilst the amount of locking required is lowest in the case of the pipeline solution, since there is a large amount of data transfer required this will probably reduce the producer–consumer concurrency except in special cases.

Another form of classification is into data communication and control communication. Although data transfer has to be controlled, control transfer includes no data. Processes may wish to pass control information, that is, just to synchronize themselves and this involves simpler communication. Semaphores are one possible mechanism on which to build more general synchronization schemes. As can be seen from the examples given earlier, the implementation is very similar to a buffer.

We have only dealt with unidirectional communication here and at the lowest level. Bidirectional communication is common in many communi-

```
DEF d=... :                     -- buffer size
CHAN w,r,intchan[d-1] :         -- read channel, write channel
                                -- and internal channels
PAR

  -- internal processes

  PAR i=[0 FOR d-2]
    VAR v :
    WHILE TRUE
      SEQ
        intchan[i]?v        -- read from input
        intchan[i+1]!v      -- write to output

  -- reader process

  WHILE TRUE
    VAR v :
    SEQ
      w?v                   -- accept from external source
      intchan[0]!v          -- send to pipeline

  -- writer process

  WHILE TRUE
    VAR v :
    SEQ
      intchan[d-2]?v        -- accept from pipeline
      r!v                   -- send to external reader

  -- interface processes

  PROC put(VALUE v)=
    w!v :
  PROC get(VAR v)=
    r?v :

  -- client processes

  PAR
    VAR x :
    ....put(x)....

    VAR y :
    ....get(y)....
```

Fig. 3.22 occam code for pipelined buffer

cation systems and this is built using two unidirectional communication channels with the appropriate protocol embedded on them. We shall, in the main, confine ourselves to unidirectional communication. Readers who wish to discover more details of bidirectional communication should consult one of the standard books on communication (for example, Tanenbaum, 1981) or a book on distributed computing (for example, Sloman and Kramer, 1987). In a later chapter we consider some of the possible higher level unidirectional communication primitives.

SUMMARY Chapter 3

In this chapter a number of different unidirectional communication schemes between a single reader and a single writer have been modelled in occam. It has been shown that a shared variable has to be represented by a encapsulated process with the synchronization constraints encoded in the encapsulated process. Another method of communication is directly between the two processes concerned. This type of communication may be unbuffered and therefore synchronized or buffered and asynchronous. For the multiple buffer case there are several possible buffer organizations, each of which has a different amount of concurrency. As well as passing data, communication channels may be used simply as a means of synchronizing a pair of processes or of providing a basic synchronization facility so that more complex synchronization schemes can be produced.

Bidirectional communication has not been dealt with here, although it can be built up using the methods presented.

EXERCISES Chapter 3

E3.1 Compare and contrast the solutions to the multi-slot buffer, Examples 9, 10 and 11? Is one more costly to implement than another?

E3.2 Can you think of any way of getting more concurrency into the buffer solution? Can you express this in occam?

E3.3 Implement a shared array in occam assuming that all elements are initialized to some known value. Repeat the exercise but this time assume that the elements of the array have to be written before being read. Repeat both these cases for the array equivalent of all the multi-slot buffer algorithms given in this chapter.

E3.4 In some real time systems it is important that the most recent data is used in computations. The buffers described in this chapter block the sender if there is no space in the buffer. In a real time system the sender would always be allowed to write to the buffer, overwriting the oldest piece of data in the buffer if it is full. If data is lost by overwriting then an indication of this would be given to the receiver(s), typically by a separate signal or by using an extra data bit. Rewrite one of the multi-slot buffer algorithms to allow this form of overwriting.

4

COMMUNICATION WITH MULTIPLE READERS AND WRITERS

The solutions described in the previous chapter for process communication only work, in general, for the case of a single producer and a single consumer. This is because only one process may read from and one write to an occam channel. To modify these examples to work for n producers and m consumers needs, in general, channel multiplexing from the producers and consumers to the resource.

4.1 GENERALIZATION TO MULTIPLE PRODUCERS AND CONSUMERS

4.1.1 Examples 1–8

We do not consider the explicit shared variable example here since it is illegal in occam. The encapsulated shared variable communication code (Example 2) given previously requires modification to Fig. 4.1 to deal with multiple readers and writers.

Here the encapsulation process has been modified so that read and write requests are accepted in any order over an array of channels rather than just a single channel.

Example 3 does not translate immediately into the multiple producer–consumer environment. We consider it in more detail in later chapters.

The modifications required to the single slot buffer example (Example 4) for multiple producers and consumers are very similar to those for Example 2. The new code required is shown in Fig. 4.2.

Note that we now need the request–receive protocol here since we do not know which output channel to use. This solution is now identical to

```
DEF n = ... :   -- number of writers
DEF m = ... :   -- number of readers
CHAN w[n],r[m],p[m] :
PAR

  -- encapsulated global variable

  VAR b :
  SEQ
    ALT i = [0 FOR n]      -- initialise buffer
      w[i]?b
        SKIP
    WHILE TRUE
      ALT                  -- note use of ALT of ALTs
        ALT i=[0 FOR n]
          w[i]?b
            SKIP
        ALT i=[0 FOR m]
          p[i]?ANY
            r[i]!b

  -- interface protocols

  PROC write(VALUE v,i)=
    w[i]!v :

  PROC read(VAR v,VALUE i)=
    SEQ
      p[i]!ANY
      r[i]?v :

  -- client processes

  PAR
    PAR i=[0 FOR n]
      VAR x :
      ....write(x,i)....

    PAR i=[0 FOR m]
      VAR y :
      ....read(y,i)....
```

Fig. 4.1 occam code for shared variable with multiple readers and writers.

that of the global variable above except for the enforcement of alternation of writing and reading.

The multi-slot buffer (Example 5) can be similarly modified and the complete solution for multiple clients is shown in Fig. 4.3.

It should be noted that these last two solutions assume a global buffer process accessible to all reader and writer processes. Solutions in which buffers are local to subsets of the readers and writers are possible and simply requires paralleling the code in Fig. 4.3 for the buffer and the client processes in the required organization.

Example 6 does not lend itself directly to the multiple reader–writer environment and solutions to the problem are considered along with those for synchronized communication in later chapters. Example 7 may be made legal by the addition of multiplexing processes as shown in Fig. 4.4.

```
DEF n = ... :   -- number of writers
DEF m = ... :   -- number of readers
CHAN w[n],r[n],p[m] :
PAR

  -- single slot buffer

  WHILE TRUE
    VAR b :
    SEQ                  -- sequentially
      ALT i=[0 FOR n] -- accept one write
        w[i]?b
          SKIP
      ALT i=[0 FOR m] -- and one read
        p[i]?ANY
          r[i]!b

  -- interface protocols

  PROC put(VALUE v,i)=
    w[i]!v :

  PROC get(VAR v,VALUE i)=
    SEQ
      p[i]!ANY
      r[i]?v :

  -- client processes

  PAR
    PAR i=[0 FOR n]
      VAR x :
      ....put(x,i)....

    PAR i=[0 FOR m]
      VAR y :
      ....get(y,i)....
```

Fig. 4.2 occam code for single slot buffer with multiple readers and writers.

Notice that the modifications to the semaphore process assume that the process acquiring the semaphore has to release it before another process can acquire it.

In a similar fashion Example 8, the general semaphore may be generalized to multiple acquire and release processes (see Fig. 4.5).

4.1.2 Example 9 – multi-slot buffer with separate index processes

Modifications to the multi-slot buffer solutions using a separate index process (Examples 9 and 10) are more extensive since we have problems of ordering and synchronization. In the case of a single producer the ordering of access to the index process and the buffer is well defined; accesses occur cyclically in the sequence index followed by buffer. In the case of multiple producers the ordering of access by each producer is well defined but the ordering of access by the set of producers is not since the

```
DEF n = ... :   -- number of writers
DEF m = ... :   -- number of readers
DEF d = ... :   -- number of buffer slots
CHAN w[n],r[m],p[m] :
PAR

  -- communications buffer

  VAR h,t,k :
  SEQ
    h:=0
    t:=0
    k:=0
    WHILE TRUE
      VAR b[d] :
      ALT
        ALT i=[0 FOR n]
          k<d & w[i]?b[t]   -- empty slot?
            SEQ
              t:=(t+1)\d
              k:=k+1
        ALT i=[0 FOR m]
          k>0 & p[i]?ANY    -- full slot?
            SEQ
              r[i]!b[h]
              h:=(h+1)\d
              k:=k-1

  -- interface protocols

  PROC put(VALUE v,i)=
    w[i]!v :

  PROC get(VAR v,VALUE i)=
    SEQ
      p[i]!ANY
      r[i]?v :

  -- client protocols

  PAR
    PAR i=[0 FOR n]
      VAR x :
      ....put(x,i)....

    PAR i=[0 FOR m]
      VAR y :
      ....get(y,i)....
```

Fig. 4.3 occam code for multi-slot buffer with multiple readers and writers.

accesses by each producer may be interleaved in any order. Thus, for example, one producer may access the index process and another producer may access the index process and deposit data into the buffer before the original process deposits its data. The depositing of data into the buffer may, therefore, not be in the same order as the acquisition of a slot index. Exactly the same problem can arise with consumer processes. Whether or not these are serious problems will depend on the use of the buffer.

As well as the ordering problem described previously there is another

```
DEF n = ? :  -- number of clients
CHAN p[n],v[n] :
PAR

  -- semaphore process

  WHILE TRUE
    ALT i=[0 FOR n]
      p[i]?ANY
        v[i]?ANY

  -- interface protocols

  PROC acq(VALUE i) =
    p[i]!ANY :

  PROC rel(VALUE i) =
    v[i]!ANY :

  -- client processes

  PAR i=[0 FOR n]
    SEQ
      ....acq(i)....rel(i)....
```

Fig. 4.4 occam code for binary semaphore with multiple readers and writers.

```
DEF n = ? :  -- number of clients
DEF d = ?? : -- max value of semaphore
CHAN p[n],v[n] :
PAR

  -- semaphore process

  VAR k :
  SEQ
    k := 0
    WHILE TRUE
      ALT i=[0 FOR n]
        k<d & p[i]?ANY  -- acq request
          k := k + 1
        k>0 & v[i]?ANY  -- req to release
          k := k - 1

  -- interface protocols

  PROC acq(VALUE i) =
    p[i]!ANY :

  PROC rel(VALUE i) =
    v[i]!ANY :

  -- client processes

  PAR i=[0 FOR n]
    SEQ
      ....acq(i)....rel(i)....
```

Fig. 4.5 occam code for general semaphore with multiple readers and writers.

```
DEF n = ... :  -- number of writers
DEF m = ... :  -- number of readers
DEF d = ... :  -- number of buffer slots
CHAN pw[n],vw[n],pr[m],vr[m],xw[n],xr[m],recxw[n],depxr[m],
     depxw[n],recxr[m] :
VAR b[d] :
PAR

  -- communications buffer

  PAR
    VAR k,l,j :
    SEQ
      k:=0          -- no of buffer full slots
      l:=0          -- no of writing slots allocated
                    -- but not yet used
      j:=0          -- no of reading slots allocated
                    -- but not yet used
      WHILE TRUE
        ALT
          ALT i=[0 FOR n]
            (k+l)<d & pw[i]?ANY    -- req to write and
                                  -- slot empty
              l:=l+1              -- slot allocated
            vw[i]?ANY             -- end of write
              SEQ
                k:=k+1            -- update slot count
                l:=l-1            -- decrement allocation
          ALT i=[0 FOR m]
            (k-j)>0 & pr[i]?ANY    -- req to read and
                                  -- full slot avail
              j:=j+1              -- slot allocated
            vr[i]?ANY             -- end of read
              SEQ
                k:=k-1            -- decrement slot count
                j:=j-1            -- decrement allocation
    -- write index
    VAR count,slotno[d] :
    SEQ
      SEQ i=[0 FOR d]
        slotno[i]:=i        -- initially all slots can be written
      count := d
      WHILE TRUE
        ALT
          ALT i=[0 FOR n]
            recxw[i]?ANY          -- request for a write slot no.
              SEQ
                xw[i]!slotno[count-1]
                count := count - 1
            depxw[i]?slotno[count]  -- return of slot no.
              count := count + 1
    -- read index
    VAR count,slotno[d] :
    SEQ
      count := 0                  -- initially no read slots
      WHILE TRUE
        ALT
          ALT i=[0 FOR m]
            recxr[i]?ANY          -- request for read slot no.
              SEQ
                xr[i]!slotno[count-1]
                count := count - 1
            depxr[i]?slotno[count]  -- return of slot no
              count := count + 1

  -- interface protocols
```

```
PROC put(VALUE v,i)=
  VAR j :
  SEQ
    pw[i]!ANY                 -- req to write
    recxw[i]!ANY              -- req write slot no
    xw[i]?j                   -- obtain slot no
    b[j]:=v                   -- write to slot
    depxr[i]!j                -- put index back into read set
    vw[i]!ANY  :              -- signal end of write

PROC get(VALUE i,VAR v)=
  VAR j :
  SEQ
    pr[i]!ANY                 -- req to read
    recxr[i]!ANY              -- req read slot no
    xr[i]?j                   -- obtain slot no
    v:=b[j]                   -- read from buffer
    depxw[i]!j                -- put index back into write set
    vr[i]!ANY  :              -- signal end of read

-- client processes

PAR
  PAR i=[0 FOR n]
    VAR x :
    ....put(x,i)....

  PAR i=[0 FOR m]
    VAR y :
    ....get(y,i)....
```

Fig. 4.6 occam code for multi-slot buffer with multiple readers and writers and separate index processes.

problem with generalizing Example 9 to multiple producers and consumers. In the single producer–consumer example, only a single counter was required to count the number of slots in use. The request for use of the buffer was dependent on the value of the count of slots in use but this is only updated after a slot is read or written. In the multiple producer–consumer case, multiple readers or writers may attempt to access the buffer concurrently and hence an access may take place when a slot is only partially in use, that is, it has been allocated but not used yet. This is unsafe as a producer or consumer process may attempt to write or read to a slot which is not empty or full, respectively. To solve this problem we introduce two more counters to count the number of read and write slots which have been allocated but not used at present. The modifications to the buffer process ensure that access is only granted if there is a slot available, that is, it now counts not only those slots used but also those partially in use, via j and l.

A further problem concerns the ordering of allocation of slots. In the single producer–consumer example it is known that the slots are filled and emptied in sequence, that is, the order of request for a slot and the order of filling or emptying slots is identical. This is not the case for multiple producers and consumers since, as we have seen in Fig. 4.5, the ordering may differ. Because of this it is not sufficient to allocate slots sequentially;

they must be allocated in the order they are used. To do this we introduce a list of full and empty slot numbers in the read and write index processes. As before the buffer process determines whether it is possible to read or write to the buffer. The write index process keeps a list of free slot numbers and a producer claims one of these if the buffer process allows him to write. After the slot has been used the producer deposits the used slot number into the list kept by the read index process. A similar set of operations occurs for the consumer except that it obtains a slot number from the read index process and returns it to the write index process (see Fig. 4.6).

As mentioned previously, this solution does *not* guarantee that the buffer is order preserving. There is no guarantee that the first reader/writer, that is, the first one to request permission to read or write via pw or pr, is the first to do xw or xr or to read to or write from the buffer. If this is required then all the code needs to be placed inside the ALT construct in the buffer to ensure the correct scheduling. Preserving the ordering by these means reduces the overall concurrency. This solution is illegal in occam for the same reason given for the single producer and consumer, namely that the global variable b is accessed for both reading and writing. This solution is, however, safe since the required synchronization constraints are built into the occam code. Encapsulating the global buffer b as a process would make the code legal.

4.1.3 Example 10 – multi-slot buffer as an array of separate slots

The multi-slot buffer (Example 10) as an array of single slot buffers works for multiple readers and writers except for the addition of multiplexing code on the access channels. The complete solution for this is shown in Fig. 4.7.

This solution does not preserve the ordering either. The ordering of obtaining a slot index and depositing/removing from the slot by a process is not guaranteed to occur before any other access to a slot. Again, to ensure that it is, means that the buffer should be made into a single process, that is, the concurrency should be reduced.

4.1.4 Example 11 – pipelined buffer

The multi-slot buffer (Example 11) implemented by a queue of processes can also be generalized to cope with multiple producers and consumers by adding multiplexing as shown in Figs. 4.8 and 4.9. Here the ordering of data into and out of the buffer is preserved since the buffer acts as a queue.

```
DEF n = ... :  -- number of writers
DEF m = ... :  -- number of readers
DEF d = ... :  -- number of buffer slots
CHAN w[d],r[d],xw[n],xr[m],recxw[n],recxr[m] :
  PAR

  -- communication buffers

    PAR
      PAR i=[0 FOR d]
        VAR b :
        WHILE TRUE
          SEQ
            w[i]?b
            r[i]!b
    -- write index
    VAR t :
    SEQ
      t:=0
      WHILE TRUE
        ALT i=[0 FOR n]
          recxw[i]?ANY
            SEQ
              xw[i]!t
              t:=(t+1)\d
    -- read index
    VAR h :
    SEQ
      h:=0
      WHILE TRUE
        ALT i=[0 FOR m]
          recxr[i]?ANY
            SEQ
              xr[i]!h
              h:=(h+1)\d

  -- interface protocols

  PROC put(VALUE v,i)=
    VAR j :
    SEQ
      recxw[i]!ANY    -- request index
      xw[i]?j         -- receive index
      w[j]!v :        -- write value

  PROC get(VAR v,VALUE i)=
    VAR j :
    SEQ
      recxr[i]!ANY    -- request index
      xr[i]?j         -- receive index
      r[j]?v :        -- read value

  -- client processes

  PAR
    PAR i=[0 FOR n]
      VAR x :
      ....put(x,i)....

    PAR i=[0 FOR m]
      VAR y :
      ....get(y,i)....
```

Fig. 4.7 occam code for multi-slot buffer as an array of single slots with multiple readers and writers and separate index processes.

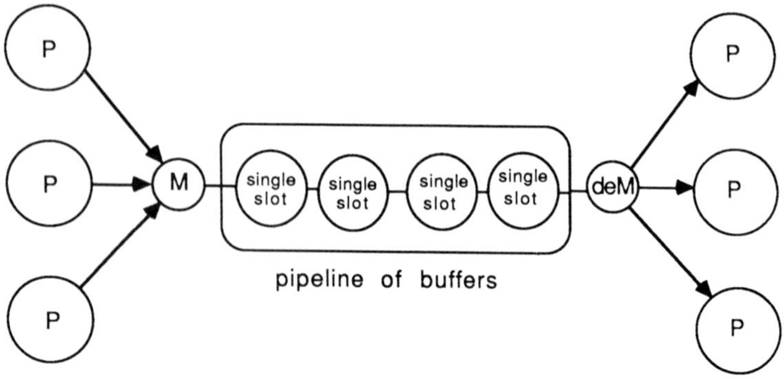

Fig. 4.8 Pipelined buffer in multiple reader/writer environment.

```
DEF n = ... :  -- number of writers
DEF m = ... :  -- number of readers
DEF d = ... :  -- number of buffer slots
CHAN w[n],p[m],r[m],intchan[d-1] :
PAR
  -- internal processes

  PAR i=[0 FOR d-2]
    WHILE TRUE
      VAR v :
      SEQ
        intchan[i]?v
        intchan[i+1]!v
  -- reader process
  WHILE TRUE
    VAR v :
    ALT i=[0 FOR n]
      w[i]?v
        intchan[0]!v
  -- writer process
  WHILE TRUE
    VAR v :
    SEQ
      intchan[d-2]?v
      ALT i=[0 FOR m]
        p[i]?ANY
          r[i]!v

  -- interface protocols

  PROC put(VALUE v,i)=
    w[i]!v :

  PROC get(VAR v,VALUE i)=
    SEQ
      p[i]!ANY
      r[i]?v :

  -- client processes

  PAR i=[0 FOR n]
    VAR x :
    ....put(x,i)....

  PAR i=[0 FOR m]
    VAR y :
    ....get(y,i)....
```

Fig. 4.9 occam code for pipelined buffer with multiple readers and writers.

SUMMARY Chapter 4

In this chapter we have seen how the channel restrictions of the occam language mean that the solutions of the previous chapter have to be modified for multiple readers and writers. Although most of the modifications are relatively straightforward, those to Example 9 are not and some of the problems encountered are not at all obvious on at a first glance. As we have seen in several of the solutions, gains in concurrency are at the expense of ordering which may or may not be important depending on the use of the communication scheme. In a later chapter we shall explore modifications to the basic occam synchronized input–output to alleviate some of the problems encountered here.

EXERCISES Chapter 4

E4.1 What is the difference in the amount of concurrency in the solutions to Examples 9, 10 and 11 for multiple clients? If the ordering of access to the buffer has to be preserved, which solution would you choose to use and why?

E4.2 Modify your answer to Exercise 3 from Chapter 3 to take account of multiple producers and consumers.

5

MORE COMMUNICATION WITH MULTIPLE READERS AND WRITERS

In the previous chapter we saw some methods of communicating between multiple anonymous senders and receivers, for example, via a buffer. In this chapter we will consider the case of Exercise 3, synchronized communication, between multiple senders and receivers. We cannot use a single occam channel since this may not be shared between multiple senders and receivers.

5.1 SIMPLE SOLUTION

The simplest solution would appear to be to add multiplexers and demultiplexers to connect the channels from each sender and receiver together but this requires the use one or more extra processes (Fig. 5.1).

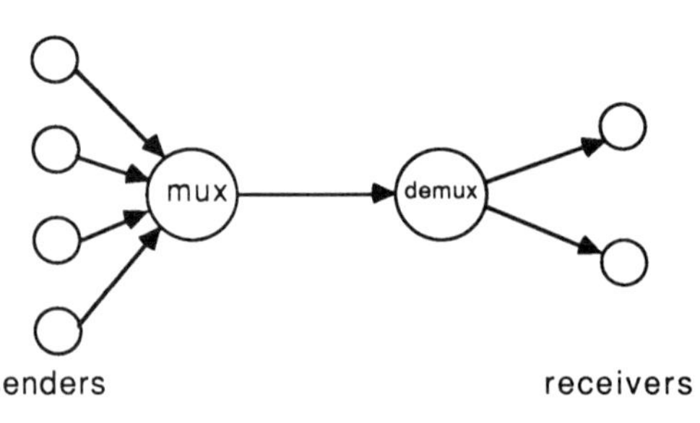

Fig. 5.1 Simple communication model.

Since it is not possible to directly couple process inputs to outputs this extra process performing the multiplexing must buffer the communication, hence giving the same solution as the single slot buffer given in the last chapter. This solution is not synchronous since the sender and receiver are decoupled by the buffer. To produce a synchronous solution we need to directly couple the senders and receivers and, since all connections are possible, we need to connect all senders to all receivers. Assuming that processes are anonymous we need a scheduler to decide which channel the sender and receiver are to use at any one time. This is the crossbar switch solution given below in the next section. Another possible solution is to use the multiplexed data path shown above but to include acknowledgement paths between receivers and senders. This could be provided by the same multiplex–demultiplex solution but in the opposite direction as shown in Fig. 5.2.

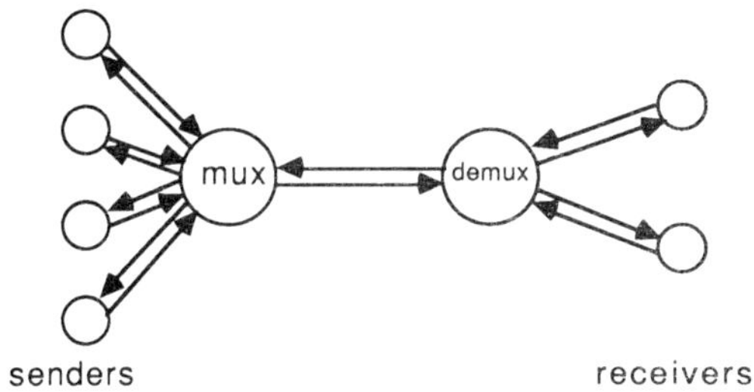

Fig. 5.2 Simple communication model with acknowledgements.

Each sender would then have to explicitly send a message followed by a wait for the reply and similarly the receiver would have to wait for a message and then send a reply. This technique of sending and immediately waiting for a reply by the sender and waiting for a message and then immediately sending a reply by the receiver may be used to provide synchronous communication between a sender and receiver with any number of intervening processes.

5.2 CROSSBAR SWITCH

In this case the *n* consumers and *m* producers are totally connected and there is a central scheduler with links to both producers and consumers which determines which connections are made (Fig. 5.3).

Communication between producer and consumer could take place along the channels to the scheduler, thus reducing the number of channels required, but this would cause a bottleneck in the scheduler and communication would be asynchronous Thus the solution we adopt is for

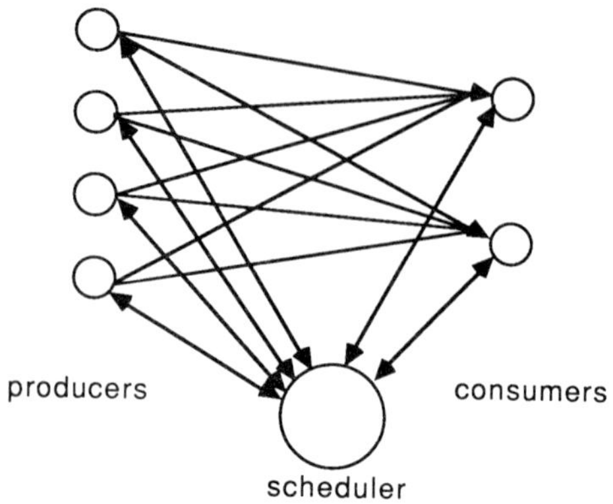

Fig. 5.3 Crossbar switch.

```
DEF n = ... :  -- number of writers
DEF m = ... :  -- number of readers
DEF nxm = n*m :  -- number of crossconnections
CHAN pconnectionreq[n],pconnection[n],  cconnection[m],
  cconnectionreq[m],crossconnection[nxm] :
PAR

  -- scheduler

  WHILE TRUE
    VAR x, i, j :
    SEQ
      ALT k=[0 FOR n]
        pconnectionreq[k]?ANY -- accept producer req
          i := k
      ALT k=[0 FOR m]
        cconnectionreq[k]?ANY  -- accept consumer req
          j := k
      -- calc x from i and j  -- calc channel to use
      -- for example x:=(i*m)+j
      pconnection[i]!x        -- inform producer
      cconnection[j]!x        -- inform consumer

  -- producers

  PAR i=[0 FOR n]
    WHILE TRUE
      VAR x :
      SEQ
        pconnectionreq[i]!ANY -- request connection
        pconnection[i]?x      -- accept channel id
        -- use link crossconnection[x]
          .
          .

  -- consumers

  PAR i=[0 FOR m]
    WHILE TRUE
      VAR x :
      SEQ
        cconnectionreq[i]!ANY  -- request connection
        cconnection[i]?x       -- accept channel id
          .
          .
```

Fig. 5.4 occam code for crossbar switch.

the communication between producer and consumer to occur via direct links (Fig. 5.4).

The maximum parallelism here is $m+n$ since n producers and m consumers can be active simultaneously.

Modifying this solution so that a producer communicates with a specific consumer obviates the need for a centralized scheduler. The producer is connected to every consumer so communicating with a specific consumer is simply a matter of output channel selection by the producer. The consumer does not know which channel the next input will arrive on, hence the need to use an ALT construct for input. The occam code for communicating with a specific consumer is shown in Fig. 5.5.

```
DEF n = ... :   -- number of writers
DEF m = ... :   -- number of readers
DEF nxm = n*m : -- number of crossconnections
CHAN crossconnection[nxm] :
PAR

  -- producers

  PAR i=[0 FOR n]
    WHILE TRUE
      VAR x,v  :
      SEQ
          .
          .
        crossconnection[x]!v

  -- consumers

  PAR i=[0 FOR m]
    WHILE TRUE
      VAR x :
      ALT j=[(i*n) FOR n]
        crossconnection[j]?x
          SKIP
```

Fig. 5.5 occam code for crossbar switch with specific consumer.

This solution, however, only works for a single transaction as the consumer may interleave reads on different channels. If the producer wishes to send a message consisting of several transactions then extra protocol is necessary. There are two solutions; either an end-of-message marker has to be added to the message or an extra channel has to be added between each producer and consumer to signal the end of transition. Since the signal follows the sending of data it can be simply sent as the last item of data providing that some special bit pattern is reserved for it. This solution may be coded as in Fig. 5.6.

A similar solution will work for multiple transactions on the general crossbar example.

```
DEF n = ... :   -- number of writers
DEF m = ... :   -- number of readers
DEF nxm = n*m :  -- number of crossconnections
DEF marker = ?  :  -- message terminator
CHAN crossconnection[n*m] :
PAR

  -- producers

  PAR i=[0 FOR n]
    WHILE TRUE
      VAR x,v  :
      SEQ
        eom := FALSE
        WHILE NOT(eom)
            .
            .
          crossconnection[x]!v
        crossconnection[x]!marker

  -- consumers

  PAR i=[0 FOR m]
    WHILE TRUE
      VAR x, eom :
      SEQ
        eom := FALSE
        ALT j = [i*n FOR n]    .
          crossconnection[i] ? x
            WHILE eom
              SEQ
                IF
                  x=marker
                    eom := TRUE
                  TRUE
                    .
                    crossconnection[i] ? x
```

Fig. 5.6 occam code for crossbar switch with specific consumer and multiple transactions.

5.3 COURIER

We now consider the case where producers and consumers are not directly connected. One method of indirect connection is the buffer as we have seen previously. However, this is a static method of indirect communication and hence the pattern of communication must be able to be predicted in advance. Instead of this method we can connect producer and consumer via a courier which acts as an active buffer, and carries information from the producer to the consumer. It has the advantage of the connections being dynamic so that the system can adapt to changes in communication patterns or those cases where the pattern cannot be predicted in advance. The simplest way to think of it is as two of the crossbar switch examples back to back with the couriers in the middle. Another way of considering the couriers is as a pool of buffers which the producers contend for (Fig. 5.7).

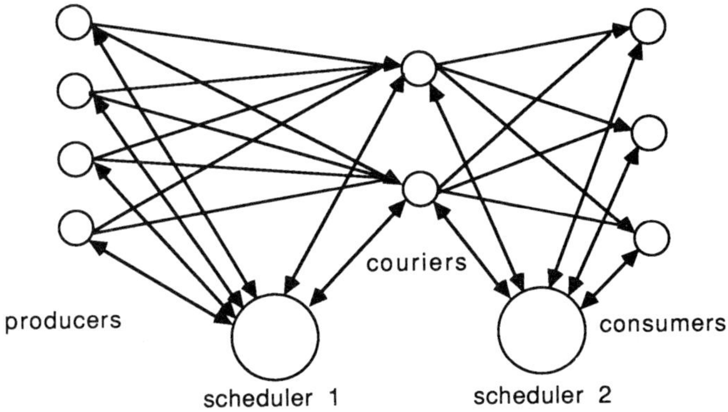

Fig. 5.7 Courier model.

In this example the assumptions are:

no. of couriers=c,
channel names are constructed from the first letter of the source, to, and the destination, e.g. ptoc .

In the courier system the maximum concurrency is $n+m(+c)$. As was the case with the crossbar example, the courier example only works for single items of data since there is no guarantee than consecutive data items from one producer will be carried to the same consumer. To obtain a solution to the message passing problem we could adopt one of two possibilities. We could set up a route and then use this route exclusively to send the complete message to the consumer, deallocating the route at the end of the message. This is known as **circuit switching**. Alternatively we could buffer the complete message in the courier and only pass it on after receiving the end of message. This is known as message switching. Another possible technique would be to allow the sender to send his message split up into small units and to add sufficient control information to each unit to allow the receiver to reconstitute the message from the small units. This is known as **packet switching**. Implementing this latter technique needs one of the other techniques since only a single item of data can be sent by the original solution. We therefore ignore this alternative at present. Implementing either of the first two techniques using the courier example is simple. We need to define an end-of-message marker and then modify the sending and receiving code in producers, consumers and couriers to loop until the end-of-message marker is sent or received.

The circuit switched solution is also a simple modification to the courier example. Changing the order of requests to the schedulers and data transfer in the courier process to that shown in Fig. 5.9 sets up the route

```
DEF n = ... :  -- number of writers
DEF m = ... :  -- number of readers
DEF c = ... :  -- number of couriers
DEF nxc = n*c :  -- number of writer-courier channels
DEF cxm = c*m :  -- number of courier-reader channels
CHAN  ptoc[nxc], ctoc[cxm], ptos[n], stoc[c], ctos[n],
  stocon[m], ptosreq[n], stocreq[c],ctosreq[c],stoconreq[m] :
PAR

  -- scheduler 1

  WHILE TRUE
    VAR x, i, j :
    SEQ
      ALT k=[0 FOR n]
        ptosreq[k]?ANY  -- accept producer req
          i := k
      ALT k=[0 FOR c]
        stocreq[k]?ANY  -- accept courier req
          j := k
      -- calc x from i and j
      ptos[i]!x
      stoc[j]!x

  -- scheduler 2

  WHILE TRUE
    VAR x, i, j :
    SEQ
      ALT k=[0 FOR c]
        ctosreq[k]?ANY  -- accept courier req
          i := k
      ALT k=[0 FOR m]
        stoconreq[k]?ANY -- accept consumer req
          j := k
      -- calc x from i and j
      ctos[i]!x
      stocon[j]!x

  -- producers

  PAR i=[0 FOR n]
    WHILE TRUE
      VAR x :
      SEQ
        ptosreq[i]!ANY      -- request connection
        ptos[i]?x
        -- use ptoc[x]
           .
           .
  -- consumers

  PAR i=[0 FOR m]
    WHILE TRUE
      VAR x :
      SEQ
        stoconreq[i]!ANY   -- request connection
        stocon[i]?x
        -- use ctoc[x]
           .
           .

  -- couriers

  PAR i=[0 FOR c]
    WHILE TRUE
      VAR x,y,z :
```

```
SEQ
  stocreq[i]!ANY   -- req sched 1
  stoc[i]?x        -- accept channel id
  ptoc[x]?z        -- copy data
  ctosreq[i]!ANY   -- req sched 2
  ctos[i]?y        -- accept channel id
  ctoc[y]!z        -- send data
```

Fig. 5.8 occam code for courier model.

initially. If we now make the same modifications as in the datagram solution for looping over a set of data items then we shall keep the same connections for the complete transaction.

```
PAR i=[0 FOR c]
 WHILE TRUE
   VAR x,y,z :
   SEQ
     stocreq[i]!ANY
     stoc[i]?x
     ctosreq[i]!ANY
     ctos[i]?y
     ptoc[i]?z
     ctoc[i]!z
```

Fig. 5.9 occam code for circuit switched courier.

Communication between a source and a designated destination does not require the second scheduler, the courier can calculate the channel to the consumer from the destination given by the producer.

This solution only works for single transactions since the destination acts as a multiplexer, that is, it will accept input from any courier. To accept multiple transactions from a single producer similar modifications to those given above are required.

The courier example also shows another problem which can occur when a particular destination is specified. If the required destination is busy then a courier is tied up with data which it cannot send. This will occur in the anonymous case also but it is not important there since the fact that no consumers are ready means that the whole system is busy whilst in the case of a specific destination it simply means that that destination is busy; other destinations may be free. Thus a single destination being overloaded could affect the performance of the whole system. To overcome this is a quite difficult problem. The courier must not commit itself to a particular producer since the required consumer may be busy. Equally the courier must not commit itself to a particular consumer since that consumer may have no producers wishing to communicate with it. We could solve the problem by letting the courier poll the producer and consumer but this is inefficient; we require a solution which does not store too much information and does not poll. The solution is to allow a courier to receive the destination required from

```
DEF n = ... :  -- number of writers
DEF m = ... :  -- number of readers
DEF c = ... :  -- number of couriers
DEF nxc = n*c :  -- number of writer-courier channels
DEF cxm = c*m :  -- number of courier-reader channels
CHAN  ptoc[nxc], ctoc[cxm], ptos[n], stoc[c], ctos[n],
  stocon[m], ptosreq[n], stocreq[c],ctosreq[c],stoconreq[m] :
PAR

  -- producer scheduler

  WHILE TRUE
    VAR x, i, j :
    SEQ
      ALT k=[0 FOR n]
        ptosreq[k]?ANY
          i := k
      ALT k=[0 FOR c]
        stocreq[k]?ANY
          j := k
      -- calc x from i and j
      ptos[i]!x
      stoc[j]!x

  -- producers

  PAR i=[0 FOR n]
    WHILE TRUE
      VAR x :
      SEQ
        ptosreq[i]!ANY
        ptos[i]?x
        -- use ptoc[x] to send dest then message
            .
            .
  -- consumers

  PAR i=[0 FOR m]
    WHILE TRUE
      VAR x :
      ALT j=[(i*c) FOR c] -- receive from any courier
        ctoc[j]?x
          SKIP

  -- couriers

  PAR i=[0 FOR c]
    WHILE TRUE
      VAR x,y,z :
      SEQ
        stocreq[i]!ANY
        stoc[i]?x
        ptoc[x]?dest
        ptoc[x]?z
        -- calc y from dest
        y := (c * dest) + i
        ctoc[y]!z
```

Fig. 5.10 occam code for courier model with specific consumer.

```
DEF n = ... :  -- number of writers
DEF m = ... :  -- number of readers
DEF c = ... :  -- number of couriers
DEF nxc = n*c :  -- number of writer-courier channels
DEF cxm = c*m :  -- number of courier-reader channels
CHAN  ptoc[n*c], ctoc[c*m], ptos[n], stoc[c], ctos[n],
  stocon[m], ptosreq[n], stocreq[c],ctosreq[c],stoconreq[m] :
PAR

  -- producer scheduler

  WHILE TRUE
    VAR x,i :
    SEQ
      ALT
        ALT k=[0 FOR n]
          ptosreq[k]?ANY
            -- search for least busy courier
            -- and store channel no in x
            i := k
        ALT k=[0 FOR c]
          ctosfree[k]?ANY -- free message from courier
            -- update use count for couriers
      -- calc x from i and j
      ptos[i]!x

  -- producers

  PAR i=[0 FOR n]
    WHILE TRUE
      VAR x :
      SEQ
        ptosreq[i]!ANY
        ptos[i]?x
        -- use ptoc[x] to send dest then message
            .
            .
  -- consumers

  PAR i=[0 FOR m]
    WHILE TRUE
      VAR x :
      SEQ
        -- read next input from buffer into j
        ctocreq[j]!ANY -- req input from courier
        -- loop to receive message

  -- couriers

  PAR i=[0 FOR c]
    WHILE TRUE
      VAR x,y,z :
      ALT
        ALT j=[0 FOR n]
          ptoc[j]?dest
            -- send i to buffer for consumer[dest]
        ALT j=[0 FOR m]
          ctocfree[j]?ANY
            -- accept any offer from consumer
            -- send message from producer to
            -- consumer via ctoc[j]
            ctosfree[i]!ANY -- free mess to scheduler
```

Fig. 5.11 More efficient courier solution.

any producer. This does not commit the courier to carry the message at that time; all that it is committed to do is to carry the message at some time in the future. The courier deposits its identity into a buffer associated with the required consumer. When the consumer is free it removes the next request from the buffer and sends that courier a message denoting that it is ready for the transaction. On receipt of this message from a consumer the courier will copy the data from the producer to the consumer. At the end of the transaction the courier reports to the scheduler so that it may update its information about how busy each courier is (Fig. 5.11).

This solution is, in fact, a solution to the Bankers Algorithm and similar problems are discussed in Chapter 6, albeit with a courier inserted into the communication path.

In the solutions to the communications using couriers so far discussed we have ignored the issue of synchronization. The objective of this chapter was to investigate methods of synchronous communication between multiple senders and receivers. The general purpose courier solution does not provide synchronous communication since the courier acts as a buffer. This solution may be modified to provide synchronous communication by ensuring that the sender is not released by the courier until the receiver has received the data. This requires a handshake protocol for communication between producer and courier rather than the one used previously. The modifications to the producer and courier processes are shown in Fig. 5.12.

```
-- producers

PAR i=[0 FOR n]
  WHILE TRUE
    VAR x :
    SEQ
      ptosreq[i]!ANY       -- request connection
      ptos[i]?x
      -- use ptoc[x],wait for ack on ctop[x]
         .
         .

-- couriers

PAR i=[0 FOR c]
  WHILE TRUE
    VAR x,y,z :
    SEQ
      stocreq[i]!ANY   -- req sched 1
      stoc[i]?x        -- accept channel id
      ctosreq[i]!ANY   -- req sched 2
      ctos[i]?y        -- accept channel id
      ptoc[x]?z        -- accept data
      ctoc[y]!z        -- send data
      ctop[x]!ANY      -- send ack to sender
```

Fig. 5.12 Synchronous courier solution 2.

In the case of multiple transactions some extra protocol is needed in communications between consumer and courier to denote the end of the message. This could take the form of a count or could be another handshake signal.

SUMMARY Chapter 5

In this chapter the ways in which synchronous communication can be extended to multiple producers and consumers have been considered. One general method uses a crossbar switch where all the producers and consumers are directly connected to one another and also to a scheduler which arbitrates on multiple concurrent requests for a single consumer. A second general method used a set of couriers, active buffers, to carry the communication from producer to consumer. In this case handshake signals are required to produce synchronous communication between producers and consumers.

EXERCISES Chapter 5

E5.1 The courier solution to communication between processes has been discussed in this chapter. What is the difference between the multi-slot buffer described in the previous chapter and the courier solution of this chapter? In what circumstances would you prefer the courier solution and why?

E5.2 If, for some physical limitation, you were restricted to implementing communication between a set of senders and receivers via a maximum of two channels how would you do it? How does this restrict the concurrency of the solution?

6

COMMUNICATION AMONGST PHYSICALLY DISTRIBUTED SYSTEMS

So far we have considered communication between **virtually distributed processes**, that is, where the processes have separate address spaces although they may exist in the same physical memory. When the processes are physically separated then communication may have to take place through a chain of processes, rather than by direct communication. In this chapter we consider some typical forms of indirect communication.

In the previous chapters we saw how indirect communication could be implemented via buffers and we saw how circuit switched and datagram communication could be implemented between a set of producers and consumers coupled via a set of couriers. In this chapter we extend the decoupling to many nodes and we illustrate some other network communication schemes.

6.1 DISTRIBUTION

6.1.1 Packet Switching

In this form of communication a message is divided into one or more packets, each of which contains routeing information and some or all of the message. The individual packets are routed through the network and the message is reassembled at the destination. The details of the routeing depend on the type of network being used.

Here we will consider a ring, one of the simplest network topologies. A ring consists of a set of nodes which are connected together in a closed loop. Each node is connected to its two nearest neighbours and to one or more hosts. Typically, communication between hosts takes the form of packets which consist of a minimum of packet destination and data. On arrival at a node a packet is sent either around the ring or to one of the hosts attached to the node if that is the destination of the packet. Hence the node acts solely as a switch. Communication around the ring is normally unidirectional.

We start by giving the code for a simple ring structure. Each host is connected to the node by two channels, inhost and outhost, and each node is connected to its neighbour by two channels, in and out (Fig. 6.1).

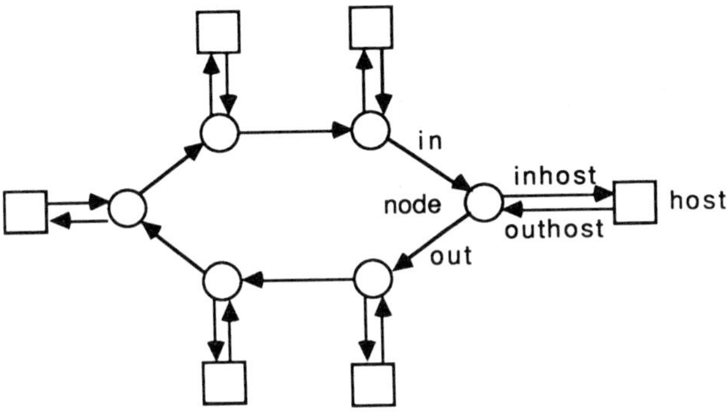

Fig. 6.1 Simple ring structure.

In this example, each node is connected to a single host. The packet format is as shown in Figs 6.2 and 6.3.

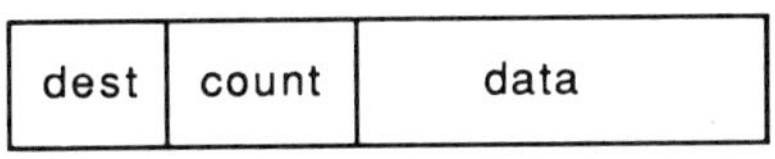

Fig. 6.2 Packet structure.

This code is sequential, that is, the node can only deal with a single packet from a single destination at a time.

A more general node can be constructed which switches between any of *n* input and *m* output channels. The code for this example is shown in Fig. 6.4.

In this solution the output channels are some function of the destination and this mapping, in a real system, would probably be performed by table lookup.

The previous two solutions allow no concurrency, that is, no interleaving of packets. In packet switching systems, where the topology may be more complex than a ring, there is often a requirement for a node to deal with several packets from different sources simultaneously. In order to do this we need to change our solution so that we have one

```
PROC node(CHAN in,out,inhost,outhost,VALUE hostid)=
  WHILE TRUE
    VAR dest,count,char :
    ALT
      hostin?dest
        SEQ
          out!dest
          inhost?count
          out!count
          SEQ i=[0 FOR count]
            inhost?char
            out!char
      in?dest
        SEQ
          IF
            dest=hostid
              SEQ
                outhost!dest
                in?count
                outhost!count
                SEQ i=[0 FOR count]
                  in?char
                  outhost!char
            dest<>hostid
              SEQ
                out!dest
                in?count
                out!count
                SEQ i=[0 FOR count]
                  in?char
                  out!char :
```

Fig. 6.3 occam code for packet switched ring node.

```
PROC node(CHAN in[],out[],VALUE n)=
  WHILE TRUE
    VAR dest,count,char :
    ALT i=[0 FOR n]
      in[i]?dest
        SEQ
          out[fn(dest)]!dest
          in[i]?count
          out[fn(dest)]!count
          SEQ j=[0 FOR count]
            in[i]?char
            out[fn(dest)]!char :
```

Fig. 6.4 More general code for ring node.

process per channel, in the extreme, and internal buffers between the input and output processes (Fig. 6.5).

The processes for input and output are shown in Fig. 6.6.

The complete system consists of *n* versions of inputport and *m* versions of outputport running in parallel with *m* versions of a buffer. The buffers are associated with each output process and must be able to accept multiple transactions from a single input port as a single packet as

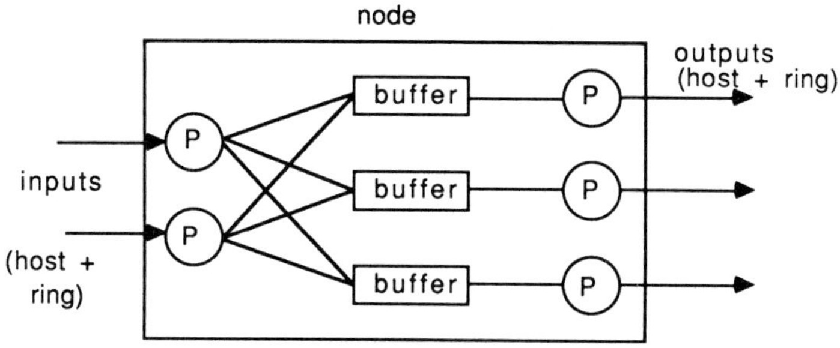

Fig. 6.5 Concurrent ring node structure.

```
PROC inputport(CHAN in,bufferin[])=
  WHILE TRUE
    VAR dest,count,char :
    SEQ
      in?dest
      bufferin[fn(dest)]!dest
      in?count
      bufferin[fn(dest)]!count
      SEQ i=[0 FOR count]
        in?char
        bufferin[fn(dest)]!char :

PROC outputport(CHAN out,bufferout)=
  WHILE TRUE
    VAR dest,count,char :
    SEQ
      bufferout?dest
      out!dest
      bufferout?count
      out!count
      SEQ i=[0 FOR count]
        bufferout?char
        out!char
```

Fig. 6.6 Basic input–output components for ring node.

described in the last chapter. Each buffer slot must be able to hold a complete packet from any input.

In the solutions discussed above the node does not store a complete packet, rather it transmits each item as it is received. In many packet switched systems the node actually stores the complete packet before transmitting it on; it acts as a store-and-forward system. This is to enable checks to be carried out to detect if there are errors in the packet and report them and destroy any incorrect packet. Fig. 6.7 illustrates a simple example of this technique, a modification of the example in Fig. 6.6.

In this example we have assumed that a process called check is available which checks the validity of the packet. In a real example the last field of a packet would be some form of checksum to enable this checking to be performed.

```
PROC node(CHAN in[],inack[],out[],outack[],VALUE n)=
  WHILE TRUE
    VAR dest,count,char[20],validity :
    ALT i=[0 FOR n]
      in[i]?dest
        SEQ
          in[i]?count
          SEQ j=[0 FOR count]
            in[i]?char[j]
          check(dest,count,char,validity)
          inack[i]!validity
          WHILE NOT(validity)   -- if not valid repeat input
            SEQ
              in[i] ? dest;count
              SEQ j = [0 FOR count]
                in[i] ? char[j]
              check(dest,count,char,validity)
              inack[i] ! validity
          validity := FALSE     -- output until received ok
          WHILE NOT(validity)
            SEQ
              out[fn(dest)]!dest;count
              SEQ j=[0 FOR count]
                out[fn(dest)]!char[j]
              outack[fn(dest)] ? validity   :
```

Fig. 6.7 Code for store and forward ring node.

6.1.2 Circuit switching

In packet switching data is sent with routeing information which allows each switch to independently route each packet to the correct destination. In circuit switching, used in the telephone system, a route, or circuit, is first established through the network and data is then transmitted along this route. After the route has been set up the nodes are configured so that no routeing information has to be sent with each packet.

We consider first a simple asymmetric network; data only flows in one direction, from source host to destination host (Fig. 6.8). This is similar to the example given in the previous section.

We have assumed that the eof token is distinct from the data in the message. If this is not the case then some extra protocol is needed, for example, an escape character to indicate non-data items in the data, or an extra channel has to be used solely for the end-of-data signal. The receiving node is terminated on receipt of an eof token.

To implement a symmetric network one possible solution is to duplicate the source and destination nodes at the opposite ends of the link and have separate channels to the host source and destination processes for sending and receiving. Thus we require two channels between every host and its associated node and between each pair of neighbouring nodes, since channels in occam are unidirectional.

```
PROC sourcenode(CHAN src,outreq[])=
  WHILE TRUE
    VAR channel,char :
    SEQ
      src?channel
      outreq[channel]!ANY
      src?char
      WHILE char<>eof
         outreq[channel]!char
         src?char
      outreq[channel]!eof :

PROC destnode(VALUE n,CHAN inreq[],dest)=
  WHILE TRUE
    ALT i=[0 FOR n]
      inreq[i]?ANY
        VAR char :
        SEQ
          inreq[i]?char
          WHILE char<>eof
            dest!char
            inreq[i]?char
          dest!eof :
```

Fig. 6.8 Code for circuit switched node.

6.2 MULTIPLE ANONYMOUS PROCESSES

In the types of distributed communication described so far it has been assumed that the sender knows the required destination. If, however, there are several destinations of the same type, any of which are acceptable to the sender, a slightly different system is required, containing some centralized arbitration and scheduling.

6.2.1 Server model

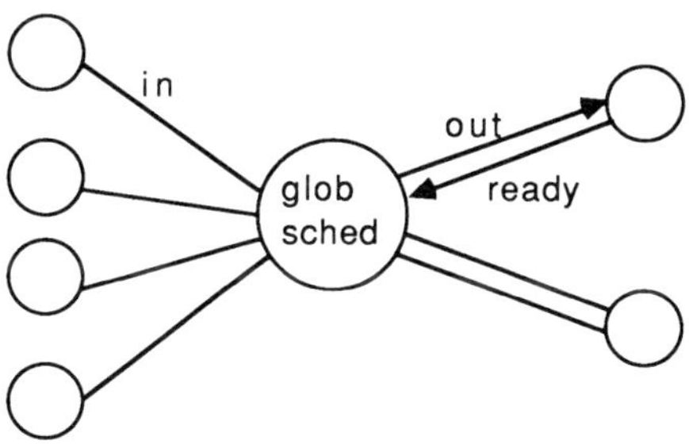

Fig. 6.9 Server model.

This solution assumes that the message sent is a single piece of data. A stream of data from a single producer may be sent to different servers.

```
PROC globscheduler(CHAN in[],out[],ready[],VALUE nin,nout)=
  WHILE TRUE
    VAR char :
    ALT i=[0 FOR nin]
      in[i]?char
        ALT j=[0 FOR nout]
          ready[j]?ANY
            out[j]!char :
```

Fig. 6.10 Code for server model scheduler.

This solution can be compared to the crossbar switch and courier solutions presented in the previous chapter. In all three cases we need centralized scheduling and we could use all three solutions for the distributed case. However, we assume that the communication costs here are high and therefore we do not wish to set up the route independently from sending the data, hence we do not use the crossbar approach. Instead we adopt a courier-like approach here but in the distributed case it is normally called a server model.

6.2.2 Stream model

This is very similar to the server case except that we need to cope with concurrent streams from separate sources, that is, all characters in a stream must go to the same server. Hence we need to remember the channel number between characters (route[i]) and we require some end-of-stream character for channel release (Fig. 6.11).

```
PROC globscheduler(CHAN in[],out[],ready[],VALUE nin,nout)=
  VAR char,route[nin] :
  SEQ
    SEQ i=[0 FOR nin]
      route[i]:=free
    WHILE TRUE
      ALT i=[0 FOR nin]
        in[i]?char
          SEQ
            IF
              route[i]=free
                ALT j=[0 FOR nout]
                  ready[j]?ANY
                    SEQ
                      out[j]!char
                      route[i]:=j
              route[i]<>free
                out[route[i]]!char
            IF
              char=eos
                route[i]:=free
              TRUE
                SKIP :
```

Fig. 6.11 Code for stream model scheduler.

This solution assumes that the server process generates ready after any stream has finished (and initially). It also assumes that the eos character indicates end of stream to the server.

These two solutions above are very similar to those given previously for the virtually distributed case since, in both cases, centralized scheduling is required. Again, in this case, characters are transferred one at a time and the amount of communication is kept as small as possible.

SUMMARY Chapter 6

In this chapter methods of communication in physically distributed systems have been considered. The two main classifications are in terms of packet switched systems in which a message is split into a number of packets, each of which is routed separately through the network, and circuit switched systems in which a route is initially set up and then data is sent along this route. The main difference between communication in physically distributed systems and virtually distributed systems is that in the former case the communication is both more costly and slower and therefore the amount of direct communication has to be reduced to a minimum.

EXERCISES Chapter 6

E6.1 In the concurrent packet system example, why is each buffer associated with an output rather than an input process?

E6.2 In the same example, would it be better to have buffers on both input and output processes? What else does this imply? Why would it be better or worse?

E6.3 What are the advantages and disadvantages of communicating with the buffer by means of a channel as opposed to a separate process?

7

SIMULATING DIGITAL LOGIC: A CASE STUDY IN occam

In previous chapters we have considered various mechanisms for communicating between a set of processes. In the next three chapters we take case studies of three problems for which we wish to program distributed solutions. In these solutions we will use some of the communication mechanisms we have previously discussed and we will illustrate some of the problems of concurrent programming discussed in Chapter 1.

It is an established practice that simulators are used as part of the design process of any complex system where it is difficult or impossible to model the system mathematically. In order to build a simulator, a model of the system behaviour is required and therefore in order to build a simulator for digital logic some form of model is required. Two different forms of model are presently in use; an event based model (Milne, 1985; Hayes, 1986) where the actions of components of the model are dependent on the occurrence of events and an axiomatic or assertional approach (Gordon, 1981; Hanna and Daeche, 1985; Moszkowski, 1983) which is a more mathematical approach and leads to the proof of system properties by formal mathematical arguments. At the present time most of the digital logic simulators are based on the former model, which we follow here, although much work is in progress on techniques using the latter approach.

Digital logic simulators have been known for many years, for example (Duley and Dietmeyer, 1968; Flake *et al.*, 1981; Hayes, 1986), but virtually all of them are implemented using a sequential programming language, with the parallelism and concurrency of the system under study being simulated. In this chapter we investigate the feasibility of using a concurrent language, specifically, occam, to see if this simplifies the design of logic simulators.

We are therefore considering distributed simulation. This is, in general, a difficult problem (Misra, 1986; Peacock, 1979) since there is no overall system clock and hence the overall state of the system is difficult to determine. In the general case events generated in one part of the system may affect the simulation in another part and, since the two parts are asynchronous, timing problems can occur. However, a digital circuit describes a static set of interconnected components and, as we shall see later, this makes the global state problem more tractable.

7.1 STRUCTURE OF A TYPICAL SIMULATOR

A typical digital simulator is event based and discrete. The input of values to any component generates an event which has a time associated with it. The processing of an event typically generates one or more events at some later time. These events are stored in a list, called an event list, and processed in time order. Thus the processing algorithm specifies that the event on the head of the list is processed, updating the global clock if necessary, and resulting events are placed at a position in the list depending on their associated time. For example, consider the circuit shown in Fig. 7.1.

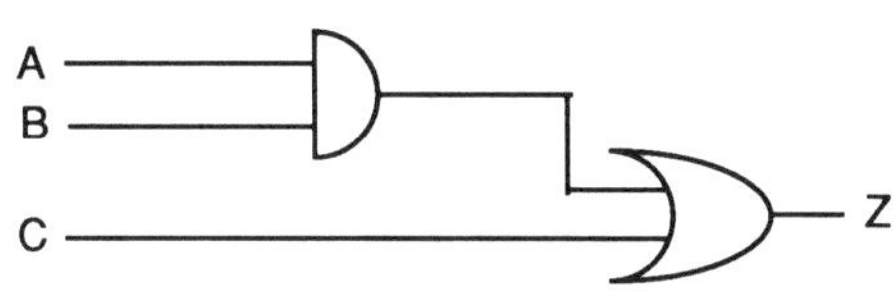

Fig. 7.1 Example circuit.

Initially no events are present in the system. Input to the circuit generates an event with that value and the time of the input, either absolute or relative to the start of the simulation. Since this is the only event at present it will be processed, that is, the action of the AND gate to which the input is attached will be simulated with this value as one of the inputs and the initial value as the other one. Processing this event may generate another event which has the output value from this component and which will cause the next component in the circuit, the OR gate, to be activated. Since there is normally a propagation delay through a component the event generated will be at a later time than the input event. This event will be placed in the queue and processed. Since there are no other events in the event queue at present this event will be processed next and will cause the simulated time to be advanced to the time of this event. Processing this event will generate a circuit output which is dealt with by the simulator as any other event except that the value will be output to the user and no other events will be generated. Other circuit inputs are dealt with in a similar manner and so events from different inputs will be processed in an order only determined by the timing of their passage through the circuit. Events happening at the same time could be processed concurrently, assuming there is no interaction between them, but the strategy outlined above is normally used in a sequential programming environment so all events are processed sequentially. We now consider how to introduce concurrency into the simulation.

7.2 THE MODEL

Instead of attempting to introduce concurrency into the event driven model we go back and consider how to model hardware with a set of concurrent processes.

The basic model of hardware is a set of processes, representing components such as gates, flip-flops and counters, and a set of communication channels representing the interconnecting wires and buses. Occam contains a process mechanism and communication channels and initial thoughts would suggest that the hardware model should map easily on to the language. However, whereas in hardware a wire maintains the logic state of the interconnection, in occam a channel does not hold a value; it simply transports a value between sender and receiver. Thus to maintain the similarity to hardware a separate process must be created to maintain the state of the interconnection or the receiver must buffer the interconnection state at its input. As we shall see later in this chapter there are many cases where the latter case suffices but occasionally a wire process is essential because of the need for buffering or for naming purposes. A further complication concerns the modelling of joined connections, fan-out and fan-in, for example, one output being connected to many inputs. In the occam model channels may only be accessed by two processes so joins have to be modelled by a separate process.

Having decided on the basic model as processes modelling components and channels modelling wires with the logic value on wires being buffered in the destination component the basic strategy of how to drive the simulation needs to be considered. There are several different strategies possible.

7.2.1 Strategy 1

The simplest strategy to adopt is a data driven strategy in which the receipt of an input causes the output to be computed and sent. This strategy can be adopted for all the components thus causing a change on the inputs to gradually percolate through the circuit model to the outputs. At the microscopic level this is how hardware actually works. However, consideration of the computational requirements leads to a less demanding strategy.

7.2.2 Strategy 2

The observation that changes in the output of a component only occur when one or more of the inputs change leads to a less computationally demanding model where only **changes** in the input values are modelled rather than the values themselves. This event driven strategy is better because less computation is involved. The processes representing components in this model accept inputs, calculate outputs and only output them if they are different from the previous value. This is exactly the model we described previously for the sequential simulator.

Here we encounter a problem which occurs using both these evaluation strategies. When an input is changed the output will change, if necessary, sometime later. How do we know that the present output of the circuit is the response to the current input, that is, that no internal processing is still being performed? In a real circuit the changes occur very quickly and often the designer relies on the fact that there is a great discrepancy between human response time and that of electronic components so that the human observer never sees intermediate results, only the final, steady state. In the simulator, however, the operations may be very much slower so outputs may lag behind inputs and we need some form of control system to tell us when the outputs are valid, that is, when they have reached their steady state value. In the sequential event driven simulator the absence of events in the event queue together with the fact that no events are being processed means that the simulator has finished processing its present input. For the concurrent case two obvious strategies come to mind; firstly, monitoring the progress of the internal computations and only reporting the circuit output when all the internal operations have finished, that is, the circuit has reached the steady state and secondly, adding some data markers so that the outputs are marked as corresponding to particular inputs. We illustrate these two strategies in the examples given later.

7.2.3 Strategy 3

The problems of determining when an output is valid suggest a further evaluation strategy based on the demand driven data flow approach to computation. In this strategy a request for output is transmitted backwards through each component of the circuit and the requested data then processed in a forwards direction. Hence input to the circuit is only performed when an output is requested. This strategy accurately reflects the timing requirements since components are not allowed to be active until all their inputs are present and hence when the final output has been received the circuit is in the steady state. Using this strategy, however, it is not possible to model some circuits. Consider the SR flip-flop circuit shown in Fig. 7.2. Here a request for Q relies on a value of Q′ and Q′ relies on Q so the requests would deadlock. While modifications are possible to overcome the problem for this circuit, in general the complications are sufficient to reject this strategy.

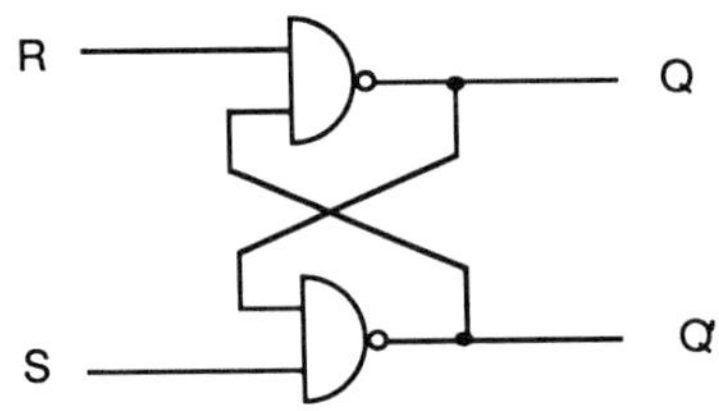

Fig. 7.2 SR flip flop.

7.3 LOGIC SIMULATION

Strategy 2, the event based one, appears to be a reasonable strategy for the simulation of logic states and is the one used in sequential simulators. Simple though this model may appear, there are problems in simulating logic circuits. The underlying occam model is asynchronous, that is, no clocking is implied and hence processes logically activated in parallel may be executed in any order. However, in the simulation of logic circuits ordering is implied since physical processes take a finite time to operate. It is the imposition of this ordering (synchronization) which is difficult in the occam model.

Consider the circuit shown in Fig. 7.1. Any change to the input variables A, B or C may affect the output value Z. In the hardware implementation, changes in the C input would be expected to change the Z output before any simultaneous change in A or B changed Z owing to the delay caused by AND gate P. However, ensuring this using occam is quite difficult since the timing constraints have to be modelled explicitly as shown later.

We now address the problem of visibility of circuit outputs. There are two options; we could constrain our model to produce outputs in exactly the same sequence as the modelled hardware or we could constrain the outputs so that they are only visible when the circuit is in its steady state. As we indicated above constraining our model to follow exactly the sequence of operations of the hardware is very difficult, even if we know what this is. Often all the designer wishes to know is what the output will be in the steady state rather than the intermediate states. Hence the exact sequence followed by the occam model does not matter provided we can detect the steady state as discussed previously.

Using the activity monitoring approach a control process may be introduced to count the number of transitions being processed at any one time. When a transition (event) enters the system a counter is incremented and when the event leaves the system the counter is decremented. When the counter returns to zero the outputs are in the steady state and may therefore be reported. Processes modelling some components increase the event count, for example, a fan out connection, some decrease the event count, for example, a multiplexer with a control input, and some will affect the event count depending on the data received, for example an AND gate.

An example of the simulation of the circuit shown in Fig. 7.1 is shown in diagrammatic form in Fig. 7.3 and the occam code given in Fig. 7.4.

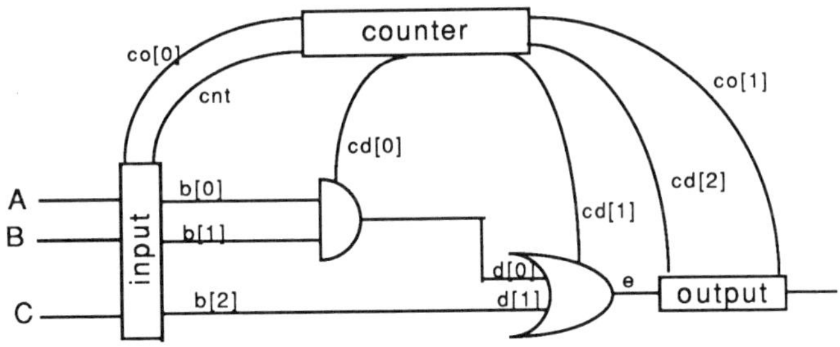

Fig. 7.3 Counter simulation of example circuit.

As shown in the diagram the control process is connected to all the other components. The channels labelled *cd* are the channels requesting the controller to count down. There are no count up channels required in this example.

In the code the AND and OR gates are modelled as described in Chapter 2. An ALT construct is used to input any transition and this value

```
--
-- occam 1 program to simulate circuit of figure 7.1
--
DEF Endbuffer = -3 :
CHAN Screen AT 1 :
CHAN Keyboard AT 2 :
--
-- process definitions
--
--
-- buffer processes
--
PROC wire(CHAN in,out)=
  VAR buffer :
  WHILE TRUE
    SEQ
      in?buffer
      out!buffer
--
-- process to simulate n input OR gate
--
PROC orgate(VALUE n,CHAN in[],out,counterdown)=
  VAR inp[n],outp :
  SEQ
    SEQ i=[0 FOR n]
      inp[i] := 0
    outp := 0
    WHILE TRUE
      VAR temp :
      SEQ
        temp := 0
        SEQ j=[0 FOR n]
          temp := temp \/ inp[j]
        IF
          temp <> outp
            SEQ
              outp := temp
              out!outp
          TRUE
            counterdown!1
        ALT i=[0 FOR n]
          in[i]?inp[i]
            SKIP   :
--
-- process to simulate n input AND gate
--
PROC andgate(VALUE n,CHAN in[],out,counterdown)=
  VAR inp[n],outp :
  SEQ
    SEQ i=[0 FOR n]
      inp[i] := 0
    outp := 0
    WHILE TRUE
      VAR temp :
      SEQ
        temp := 1
        SEQ j=[0 FOR n]
          temp := temp /\ inp[j]
        IF
          temp <> outp
            SEQ
              outp := temp
              out!outp
          TRUE
            counterdown!1
        ALT i=[0 FOR n]
          in[i]?inp[i]
```

```
            SKIP   :
--
-- process to count events
--
PROC counter(VALUE nstart,ninc,ndec,nout,CHAN incount,
             inc[],dec[],out[])=
--
-- nstart is initialised count
-- ninc is no of increment channels
-- ndec is no of decrement channels
-- nout is no of output channels
--
  VAR count :
  SEQ
    count := nstart
    WHILE TRUE
      SEQ
        WHILE count <> 0
          VAR x :
          SEQ
            ALT
              ALT i=[0 FOR ninc]
                inc[i]?x
                  SEQ
                    count := count+x
              ALT i=[0 FOR ndec]
                dec[i]?x
                  SEQ
                    count := count-x
        SEQ i=[1 FOR nout]
          out[i]!ANY
        out[0]!ANY
        incount?count
        out[0]!ANY   :
--
-- output process
--
PROC outputmodule(CHAN in,controlin,counterdown)=
  VAR lastout :
  SEQ
    lastout := 0
    WHILE TRUE
      ALT
        in?lastout
          counterdown!1
        controlin?ANY
          SEQ
            Screen!(lastout+'0')  -- convert to ASCII
            Screen!#A             -- send CR (hex 10)
            Screen!#D             -- send LF (hex 13)
            Screen!Endbuffer   :  -- flush VDU buffer
--
-- process to translate from circuit inputs to
-- transitions(events)
--
PROC inputmodule(VALUE ninp,CHAN inchar,out[],
                 controlin,counterout)=
  VAR outv[ninp]  :
  SEQ
    SEQ i=[0 FOR ninp]
      outv[i] := 0
    WHILE TRUE
      VAR trans,newval[ninp] :
      SEQ
        controlin?ANY
```

Continued

Continued

```
          trans := 0
          SEQ i=[0 FOR ninp]
            inchar?newval[i]
            IF
              newval[i] <> outv[i]
                trans := trans + 1
              TRUE
                SKIP
          counterout!trans
          controlin?ANY
          SEQ i=[0 FOR ninp]
            IF
              newval[i] <> outv[i]
                SEQ
                  outv[i] := newval[i]
                  out[i]!outv[i]
              TRUE
                SKIP   :
--
-- process to input a char from terminal
--
PROC input(CHAN outchar)=
  WHILE TRUE
    VAR character :
    SEQ
      Keyboard?character
      character := character - '0'   -- convert to no from ASCII
      outchar!character   :
--
-- channels as in figure
--
CHAN a,b[3],d[2],e,cnt,cu[3],cd[3],co[2]:
--
-- process instantiations
--
-- do processes concurrently
--
PAR
  input(a)
  inputmodule(3,a,b,co[0],cnt)
  andgate(2,b,d[0],cd[0])
  orgate(2,d,e,cd[1])
  wire(b[2],d[1])
  outputmodule(e,co[1],cd[2])
  counter(2,0,3,1,cnt,cu,cd,co)
```

Fig. 7.4 occam code for example circuit.

together with the latest values of the other inputs is used to calculate the current output. This value is only output if it is different from the last one, that is, if an output transition occurs. Any output from the circuit will only be permitted when a control signal has been received from the controller indicating that the steady state has been reached. The wire process is used to connect the output from one process to the input of another and is necessary because the AND and OR processes have been written as general purpose gates which take *n* inputs. The only method of having an indeterminate number of input channels in an occam process is to use an array of chemicals. While it is possible to do some wiring by

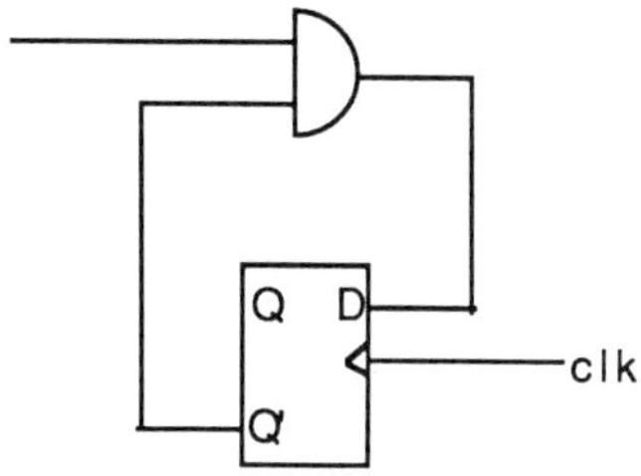

Fig. 7.5 Circuit showing deadlock.

means of the appropriate naming in process instantiations, the general case of wiring arrays of channels together can only be solved by creating separate wire processes to copy from one channel to another.

There is another reason for using wire processes. Consider the portion of code shown in Fig. 7.5. This circuit can deadlock as the AND gate can commit itself to output at the same time as the flip-flop commits itself to output. The solution to this problem is to add a buffer process in the feedback loop. This buffer process can take the form of a wire process as described previously or may be a join process dealing with fan-out or fan-in.

A further problem with the simulation concerns the initialization of the processes. Ideally all the components would assume their inputs and outputs to be in a consistent state initially. This cannot be done on a component to component basis since some components will have inputs and outputs of the same polarity whilst others will not. Thus the state of the 'wires' depends on the components connected at either end. The simulation thus has to go through an initialization phase to ensure consistency of component inputs and outputs. Initially each component assumes that its inputs and outputs are at logic state 0 and then computes a new output from this input set. If output transitions are generated then this fact is reported to the controller and the transitions sent along the output channels. Only when the results of the initialization have percolated through all the circuit does the controller allow external inputs.

The problem with the solution presented is that it is essentially a centralized approach since the global state of the system is stored in the counter. Ideally we require a more distributed approach and so we consider a data flow solution. A solution to the circuit simulation using this approach to detecting the steady state by adding markers to the data to denote the final output is given in Fig. 7.6. Here we send special flush tokens following data input to denote the end of data. The components pass on the special token at the end of their output and when the final output module receives one of these tokens on each of its input channels it knows that the steady state has been reached and that it can output its current value. In the example we have coded the flush token as a special data value but it could equally well be coded as part of the data, provided that the data representation had enough redundancy or as a separate control signal associated with each data arc. Note that we could clock the data through the complete circuit thus only allowing more input after output from the current input has been produced. Applying this principle to components rather than the complete circuit we can pipeline the data through the circuit knowing that the outputs will emerge in the order of the data inputs. The examples in Figs 7.4 and 7.6 are of a **clocked combinatorial circuit** in which the clocking is controlled by the controller process in the first case and the flush token generator in the second. Because of the nature of the simulation all the inputs to and outputs from the circuit are clocked thus making the simulation a clocked one, even for asynchronous circuits. Looking at the two examples it is obvious that the one using flush tokens is much simpler than that using a counter. As we shall see, it is not always possible to use this approach for simulation and then we have to resort to the counting approach.

Simulating sequential logic circuits is no more difficult that simulating combinatorial ones; Fig 7.7 shows the occam code for a D-type flip-flop.

There is a problem with the flush token solution here. What should the action be when a flush token is received? The normal mode of operation of a circuit with flip-flops is for the data to be changed first, followed by the clock signal, after the data has settled down. We have therefore adopted the approach that flush tokens on the data lines are ignored and those on the control lines cause flush tokens to appear on the outputs. Thus the circuit of Fig. 7.5 can be simulated using this approach. Now consider circuits with feedback. These can cause problems for simulation since we have assumed so far that incorrect events will only generate values which eventually get overwritten. However, if feedback loops are present in a circuit then the incorrect value will eventually return to a previous part of the circuit and may cause another event. Since we do not specify the order in which events are processed the feedback path may take precedence and cause indefinite looping in the simulation. The only solution to this is to add timing information as described below.

7.4 TIMING SIMULATION

Standard logic simulators produce a timing diagram as output as well as the steady state outputs and this section considers how we can do this using occam. We cannot use the same model because intermediate values

```
--
-- occam 1 program to simulate circuit of figure 7.1
-- using flush tokens
--
DEF Endbuffer = -3 :
DEF flushtoken = ... : -- unique data value for token
DEF size = ...         -- max no of gate inputs
CHAN Screen AT 1 :
CHAN Keyboard AT 2 :
--
-- process definitions
--
--
-- process to buffer two processes
--
PROC wire(CHAN in,out)=
  WHILE TRUE
    VAR buffer :
    SEQ
      in?buffer
      out!buffer
--
-- process to simulate n input OR gate
--
PROC orgate(VALUE n,CHAN in[],out)=
  VAR outp :
  SEQ
    outp := 0
    WHILE TRUE
      VAR lvalue[size],flushcount :
      SEQ
        SEQ i=[0 FOR n]
          in[i]?lvalue[i]
        flushcount := 0
        WHILE TRUE
          VAR temp :
          SEQ
            temp := 0
            SEQ i=[0 FOR n]
              temp := temp \/ lvalue[i]
            IF
              temp <> outp
                SEQ
                  outp := temp
                  out!outp
              TRUE
                SKIP
            eoi := TRUE
            WHILE eoi
              VAR val :
              ALT i=[0 FOR n]
                in[i]?val
                  SEQ
                    IF
                      val = flushtoken
                        IF
                          flushcount = (n - 1)
                            SEQ
                              out!flushtoken
                              eoi := FALSE
                              flushcount := 0
                          TRUE
                            flushcount := (flushcount+1)

                      TRUE
                        SEQ
```

Continued

Continued

```
                                lvalue[i] := FALSE
                                eoi := FALSE :
--
-- process to simulate n input AND gate
--
PROC andgate(VALUE n,CHAN in[],out)=
  VAR outp :
  SEQ
    outp := 0
    WHILE TRUE
      VAR lvalue[size],flushcount :
      SEQ
        SEQ i=[0 FOR n]
          in[i]?lvalue[i]
        flushcount := 0
        WHILE TRUE
          VAR temp :
          SEQ
            temp := 1
            SEQ i=[0 FOR n]
              temp := temp /\ lvalue[i]
            IF
              temp <> outp
                SEQ
                  outp := temp
                  out!outp
              TRUE
                SKIP
            eoi := TRUE
            WHILE eoi
              VAR val :
              ALT i=[0 FOR n]
                in[i]?val
                  SEQ
                    IF
                      val = flushtoken
                        IF
                          flushcount = n - 1
                            SEQ
                              out!flushtoken
                              eoi := FALSE
                              flushcount := 0
                          TRUE
                            flushcount := flushcount+1

                      TRUE
                        SEQ
                          lvalue[i] := FALSE
                          eoi := FALSE :
--
-- output process
--
PROC outputmodule(CHAN in)=
  WHILE TRUE
    VAR lastout :
    SEQ
      in?lastout
      IF
        lastout=flushtoken
          SEQ
            Screen!(lastout+'0')
            Screen!#A
            Screen!#D
            Screen!Endbuffer
        TRUE
          SKIP  :
```

```
--
-- process to translate from single input to
-- multiple output including flushtokens
--
PROC inputmodule(VALUE ninp,CHAN inchar,out[])=
  VAR outv[size]  :
  SEQ
    SEQ i=[0 FOR ninp]
      outv[i] := 0
    WHILE TRUE
      SEQ i=[0 FOR ninp]
        inchar?outv[i]
        out[i]!outv[i]
        out[i]!flushtoken :
--
-- process to input a char from terminal
--
PROC input(CHAN outchar)=
  WHILE TRUE
    VAR character :
    SEQ
      Keyboard?character
      character := character - '0'
      outchar!character   :
--
-- channels as in figure
--
CHAN a,b[3],d[2],e:
--
-- process instantiations
--
-- do processes concurrently
--
PAR
  input(a)
  inputmodule(3,a,b)
  andgate(2,b,d[0])
  orgate(2,d,e)
  wire(b[2],d[1])
  outputmodule(e)
```

Fig. 7.6 occam code for flush token model.

may not be correct due to the ordering problem, as discussed previously. For a timing simulation we are interested in the intermediate values and we therefore use a simple event-based data flow model for this type of simulation. Adopting this strategy does not, however, overcome the ordering problem; we need to add some extra control for this.

In our timing simulation we timestamp every piece of data input to the model. Output from any component carries the timestamp from the input with a delay modelling the component transit time. Ideally we would wish to process inputs to a component in timestamp order. This is equivalent to processing inputs in time sorted order. There is a problem in programming this since we cannot predict in which order processes instantiated in a PAR will actually be executed. Thus we cannot know if we have a data value on an input channel whether there are any values with smaller timestamps in the system which may appear at the same

```
--
-- process to simulate D type flip-flop
--
-- normal notation for flip-flop
--
-- counter model
--
PROC Dfflop(CHAN clk,d,q,qbar,inc,incack,dec,decack)=
--
-- local variables
-- dval   current state of input to ff
-- state  current state of ff
-- cval   current value of clock input
--
  VAR dval,state :
  SEQ
    dval := 0
    state := 0
    qbar!1
    WHILE TRUE
      VAR cval :
      ALT
        d?dval
          SEQ
            dec!1
            decack?ANY
        clk?cval
          SEQ
            IF
              cval = 0
                SEQ
                  dec!1
                  decack?ANY
              TRUE
                IF
                  dval<>state
                    SEQ
                      inc!1
                      incack?ANY
                      state := dval
                      q!dval
                      qbar!((dval + 1) /\ 1)
                  TRUE
                    SEQ
                      dec!1
                      decack?ANY  :
```

Fig. 7.7a occam process for D flip-flop using counter.

component at a later simulation time. We need to control two properties here. Firstly, we need to make sure that values on a channel appear in timestamp order and, secondly, we need to ensure that the inputs to a component are dealt with in timestamp order.

One solution to these problems is for each component to store the history of values it has seen and then to match up any new input value with the corresponding time values on the other inputs when calculating new outputs. Since there is no guarantee that inputs will occur in order, incorrect values may be generated because the correct information has not yet been received. As in the simulation of logic values all that can be guaranteed is that the final value for any particular timestamp will be

```
--
-- process to simulate D type flip-flop
--
-- normal notation for flip-flop
--
-- flush token model
--
PROC Dfflop(CHAN clk,d,q,qbar,inc,incack,dec,decack)=
--
-- local variables
-- dval  current state of input to ff
-- state current state of ff
-- cval  current value of clock input
--
  VAR dval,state :
  SEQ
    dval := 0
    state := 0
    qbar!1
    WHILE TRUE
      VAR cval :
      ALT
        d?x
          IF
            x<>flushtoken
              dval := x
            TRUE
              SKIP
        clk?cval
          SEQ
            IF
              cval = flushtoken
                SEQ
                  q!flushtoken
                  qbar!flushtoken
              cval = 0
                SKIP
              TRUE
                IF
                  dval<>state
                    SEQ
                      state := dval
                      q!dval
                      qbar!((dval + 1) /\ 1)
                  TRUE
                    SKIP  :
```

Fig. 7.7b occam process for D flip-flop using flush tokens.

correct. Thus the output stage of the circuit has to buffer the complete simulation and only output it when all activity in the modelled circuit has finished.

The above solution works except for solutions containing feedback but it is not very efficient. A better solution would attempt to impose an ordering on the execution of the component modules. If we are to execute the modules in the correct order we have to deal with the inputs in the correct order. Assuming that the communication over channels is in the correct time order then each component module needs only to select the earliest from an input from each input channel. To do this we need to add a special marker to the input data to indicate the end of data

```
--
-- occam 1 program for circuit of figure 7.1
-- using flush tokens for timing simulation
--
DEF Endbuffer = -3 :
DEF flushtoken = ... : -- unique data value for token
DEF maxtime = ...   : -- maximum simulation time
DEF andgate = 1,  -- type value for and
    orgate = 2  : -- type value for or
DEF andgatetime = ..., -- transit time for and
    orgatetime = ... : -- transit time for or
DEF size = ...       -- maximum no. of gate inputs
CHAN Screen AT 1 :
CHAN Keyboard AT 2 :
--
-- process definitions
--
--
-- process to buffer two processes
--
PROC wire(CHAN in,out)=
  WHILE TRUE
    VAR buffer :
    SEQ
      in?buffer
      out!buffer
--
-- process to simulate n input 1 output gates
--
PROC n.input.1.out.gate(VALUE type,n,CHAN in[],out)=
  VAR ltemp,lvalue[size] :
  SEQ
    ltemp := 0
    SEQ i =[0 FOR n]
      lvalue[i] := 0
    WHILE TRUE
      VAR val[size],time[size],outsent,flush,more :
      SEQ
        SEQ i=[0 FOR n]
          in[i]?val[i];time[i] -- values from inputs
        outsent := FALSE
        flush := 0  -- no of flush tokens recd
        more := TRUE
        WHILE more
          VAR ctime,temp :
          SEQ
            ctime := maxtime -- init maxtime
            SEQ j=[0 FOR n]
              IF
                val[j]=flushtoken
                  SKIP
                time[j]<ctime
                  SEQ
                    ctime := time[j]
                    i := j
                TRUE
                  SKIP
            lvalue[i] := val[i]
            IF
              type=andgate
                SEQ
                  temp := 1
                  SEQ j=[0 FOR n]
                    temp := temp/\lvalue[j]
                  ctime := ctime + andgatetime
              type=orgate
                SEQ
                  temp := 0
```

```
                SEQ j=[0 FOR n]
                  temp := temp\/lvalue[j]
                ctime := ctime + orgatetime
            TRUE
              SKIP
          IF
            temp <> ltemp  -- output changed
              SEQ
                outsent := TRUE
                ltemp := temp
                out!temp
                out!ctime
            TRUE
              SKIP
          in[i]?val[i]
          IF
            val[i]=flushtoken
              flush := flush + 1
            TRUE
              in[i]?time[i]
          IF
            flush=n
              SEQ
                IF
                  outsent
                    SKIP
                  TRUE
                    out!temp;ctime
                out!flushtoken
                more := FALSE
            TRUE
              SKIP :
--
-- output process
--
PROC outputmodule(CHAN in)=
  WHILE TRUE
    VAR out,time,more :
    SEQ
      more := TRUE
      in?out;time
      WHILE more
        SEQ
          Screen!(out+'0')
          -- convert time to chars and
          -- output to screen
          Screen!#A
          Screen!#D
          Screen!Endbuffer
          in?out
          IF
            out <> flushtoken
              in?time
            TRUE
              more := FALSE  :
--
-- process to translate from single input to
-- multiple output including flushtokens
--
PROC inputmodule(VALUE ninp,CHAN intime,inchar,out[])=
  VAR outv[size]  :
  SEQ
    SEQ i=[0 FOR ninp]
      outv[i] := 0
    WHILE TRUE
      VAR time :
```

Continued

Continued

```
          SEQ
            intime?time
            SEQ i=[0 FOR ninp]
              inchar?outv[i]
              out[i]!outv[i]
              out[i]!flushtoken :
--
-- process to input a char from terminal
--
PROC input(CHAN outchar)=
  WHILE TRUE
    VAR character :
    SEQ
      Keyboard?character
      character := character - '0'
      outchar!character   :
--
-- clocking process
--
PROC tick(CHAN clock)=
  VAR time :
  SEQ
    time := 0
    WHILE TRUE
      clock!time
      time := time + 1 :
--
-- channels as in figure
--
CHAN a,b[3],d[2],e,clock:
--
-- process instantiations
--
-- do processes concurrently
--
PAR
  input(a)
  inputmodule(3,clock,a,b)
  n.input.1.out.gate(andgate,2,b,d[0])
  n.input.1.out.gate(orgate,2,d,e)
  wire(b[2],d[1])
  outputmodule(e)
  tick(clock)
```

Fig. 7.8 occam code for timing solution using flush token model.

over a channel. If we assume simple components where processing time is not data dependent then, using this strategy, the outputs will be in timestamp order. Thus we know in this case that the outputs from the circuit will be produced in correct time order. In effect, in this model we are clocking the data over a particular time period and then using flush tokens on all the channels to ensure that there is a time reference point for the termination of operations at each component. We show the occam code to simulate a timing diagram for the circuit of Fig. 7.1 in Fig. 7.8.

In fact this type of timing simulation only works for some circuits. Consider the SR flip-flop of Fig. 7.2. The feedback lines to each NAND gate mean that no input on those channels will be produced until the NAND processing has been performed and this cannot take place until the feedback from the other NAND has been processed; a deadlock situation. We could overcome the problem here by initializing the feedback connections to a consistent logic value timestamped with the simulation time. The question then arises as to how to deal in general with circuits containing feedback. This is where the problem is simpler than the general distributed simulation case since we can make use of the static property of logic circuits. Any feedback in a circuit occurs over known paths which have a fixed delay and therefore the time for events to propagate around a loop may be known in advance. Thus an event generated at a component having feedback inputs can only generate events on the feedback inputs at known times. Thus the algorithm above will work for circuits with feedback provided the delay time around any feedback loops is calculated at initialization time and used to calculate the time of inputs on feedback paths. The actual code for this is not given here but is left as an exercise (E7.3) for the interested reader.

SUMMARY Chapter 7

In this chapter the modelling of digital circuits in occam has been considered. Although, on the surface, it would appear to be a problem for which occam is well suited, the modelling turns out to be more complex than expected. In fact simulation can become complex, especially if a timing diagram is required. However this example has shown that in some ways occam is a convenient language for this type of simulation in that we can express the various strategies and models in the language. However occam poses a number of problems in constructing a model which accurately reflects the timing constraints.

EXERCISES Chapter 7

E7.1 Write code for occam processes to simulate:

- **a** a divide by 3 up-down counter,
- **b** a 16x4 ROM,
- **c** a PLA with 3 input terms, 3 product terms and 2 outputs.

E7.2 Under what conditions can simulation of a network deadlock? (Hint: refer to Chapter 1.) How would you ensure than this did not happen in the simulation of a digital logic network?

E7.3 Outline the algorithm required to deal with the simulation of circuits with feedback. Program the algorithm in occam using as much concurrency as possible.

8

DATA STRUCTURES AS PROCESSES

Conventionally data structures are implemented as passive programming objects; as aggregations of units which have some structure which is used to access them. An alternative form of representation is as a collection of processes, each one representing a unit or part of the structure. We have already seen this type of representation in the case of the multi-slot buffer represented as an array of single slot buffers. Here each process represented a slot in the buffer and access to separate slots was via an index. As we saw then the advantage of such a buffer is that access can be made concurrently to the separate items in the buffer with the data integrity being conserved by internal synchronization constraints in the code to access each item. This is also true of other data structures; they may also be accessed concurrently, subject to the necessary synchronization constraints. Global synchronization, for example, to lock the complete structure, may be implemented by communication between the processes.

8.1 BINARY TREES

We illustrate the use of processes to model data structures in this chapter by modelling a binary tree structure using successively more concurrency. The only data structure in occam is a vector so the simplest way of implementing a binary tree is to map it on to a vector. There are a number of different mappings possible. For example, the children of a node, at vector position n, could be placed at positions $2n+1$ and $2n+2$ with the root node at index 0.

This would map a balanced structure with an equal number of nodes in the left and right branches. To make the structure more flexible some

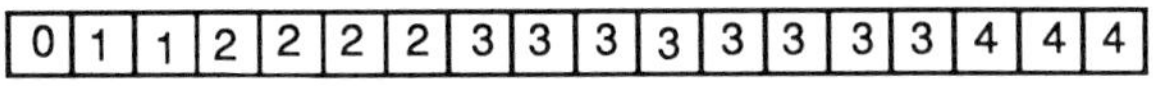

Fig. 8.1 Mapping of binary tree to a vector.

form of pointer mechanism is required. This would allow any type of unbalanced tree to be represented without a waste of space. To simulate pointers extra vectors are required as shown in Fig. 8.2.

Fig. 8.2 Simulating pointers as vectors.

We illustrate our models of a binary tree by showing how they may be accessed by operations to insert a value, check if a specified value is present and print the complete contents of the tree in preorder. For our first model we give the direct analogue of the standard sequential code but rewritten in occam. Remember that occam does not allow recursion so the normal recursive access operations cannot be used.

```
DEF empty = ... -- initial node values
DEF n = ...   -- max size of tree
VAR tree[n],rchild[n],lchild[n],free :

PROC searchi(VAR i,VALUE v)=  -- search branch of tree
  WHILE i<>empty              -- pointed at by i for
    IF                        -- free node and when
      tree[i]=empty           -- found insert v
        SEQ
          tree[i] := v
          rchild[i] := free
          lchild[i] := free + 1
          free := free + 2
          i := empty
      v<tree[i]
        i := left[i]
      TRUE
        i := right[i]   :

PROC insert(VALUE v)=         -- insert v into tree
  VAR i :
  SEQ
    IF
      tree[0]=empty
```

Continued

Continued

```
          SEQ
            tree[0] := v
            rchild[0] := free
            lchild[0] := free + 1
            free := free + 2
        v<tree[0]
          SEQ
            i := left[0]
            searchi(i,v)
        TRUE
          SEQ
            i := right[0]
            searchi(i,v)   :

PROC searchc(VALUE v,VAR reply,i)= -- search branch of
  WHILE i<>empty                   -- tree pointed at
    IF                             -- by i for value v
      tree[i]=empty                -- reply found or
        SEQ                        -- not found
          reply := FALSE
          i := empty
      tree[i]=v
        SEQ
          reply := TRUE
          i := empty
      v<tree[i]
        i := left[i]
      TRUE
        i := right[i]   :

PROC check(VALUE v,VAR reply)=  -- see if v in tree
VAR i :
  SEQ
    IF
      tree[0]=empty
        reply := FALSE
      tree[0]=v
        reply := TRUE
      v<tree[0]
        SEQ
          i := left[0]
          searchc(v,reply,i)
      TRUE
        SEQ
          i := right[0]
          searchc(v,reply,i)   :

PROC print =
  -- code not given since it is complicated
  -- links need to be changed in going down the
  -- tree to point back and to be reset after the
  -- subtree values printed

PROC init =                     -- initial state
  SEQ
    free := 1
    SEQ i=[0 FOR n]
      tree[i] := empty
      left[i] := empty
      right[i] := empty   :

SEQ
  -- client processes
```

Fig. 8.3 occam code for sequential access to binary tree.

This solution does not include any concurrency and does not check for overflow, that is, attempts to insert more than n elements in the tree. Some concurrency can be included by allowing the clients to be run in parallel with the tree processes. This implies that there may be concurrent requests for tree operations. The simplest solution here is to add an interface process between the clients and the tree to serialize the requests, thus giving the structure:

```
PAR

  -- client processes

  -- interface process
  SEQ
    ALT i=[0 FOR n]
      in[i]?op
        SEQ
  -- perform op on tree
  out[i]!reply
```

Fig. 8.4 Tree interface process.

This solution requires two channels, in and out, between the tree interface process and each client to transfer the requests for tree operations and the replies to these requests. The concurrency here is limited to client concurrency since only one access to the tree at a time is allowed. To introduce more concurrency means allowing concurrent access to the tree structure. This requires major modifications, both to allow concurrency of access to the tree and to implement the required synchronization constraints. Taking the synchronization constraints first, these can be implemented in the interface process. Operations which only read data can be performed concurrently whilst operations which write data can only be performed sequentially and not at the same time as read operations. For the operations of insertion, checking and printing this means that checking and printing can occur concurrently but in mutual exclusion to insertion. Furthermore, printing operations can only occur sequentially otherwise results of concurrent operations could be interleaved. These synchronization constraints can be implemented using suitable Boolean flags as shown in the following solution. In order that the tree structure may be accessed concurrently we need to change the tree into separate node processes each of which communicates with its neighbours via channels. Since we need to pass information both up and down the tree structure we need two channels between a node and each of its neighbours. Thus we obtain a solution such as the one shown below.

The channels linking each node to its relatives are indexed by the following scheme:

a a nodes channels to its children are indexed by

2*nodenumber + 1
and 2*nodenumber + 2

b a nodes channel to its parent is indexed by
nodenumber

as shown in the Fig. 8.5.

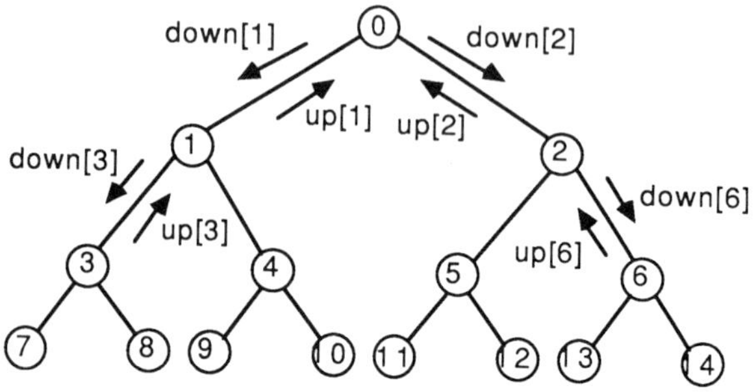

Fig. 8.5 Binary tree showing channels.

The root node, number 0, communicates with the client processes via an interface process which collects requests and passes them to the root node in an abbreviated form as shown below. This interface process is also responsible for packaging the replies to the client processes into a suitable format.

Considering the insertion operation first, we assume that the interface process will send to the root node a code indicating insertion followed by the value along the same input channel. The action of the root node of the tree for this operation is to see if it contains a value and, if not, to store the input value and acknowledge to the interface process. If the root process does contain a value then it will pass the insertion request and value to one of its children depending on whether the new value is less than or greater than its stored value. The other nodes will respond in a similar fashion so eventually the new value will be stored and an acknowledgement passed back to the interface process. There is a potential problem here; the possibility of overflow of storage because all the nodes in the required branch of the tree are occupied. We shall consider this problem in some detail later.

Turning to the second operation, checking for a given value, this is very similar to the insertion operation except that the value is compared against the stored values and, if an empty node is reached in the search then a negative reply is generated.

The final operation, printing in preorder, is slightly more complex as can be seen from the code below. In essence a print token is passed around the tree causing printing whenever it reaches a node.

```
DEF empty = ...   -- initial value held in nodes
DEF iackpos = ... -- positive response to i command
DEF cackpos = ... -- positive response to c command
DEF cackneg = ... -- negative response to c command
DEF n = ... :  -- maximum number of nodes
CHAN down[n],up[n] :
PAR
  PAR i=[0 FOR n]  -- for all the nodes in the tree
    DEF lchild = (2*i) + 1 :   -- left child pointer
    DEF rchild = lchild + 1 :-- right child pointer
    VAR val :
    SEQ
      val := empty      -- initial value of node
      WHILE TRUE
        VAR v,ans,cmnd
        SEQ
          ALT               -- accept input
            down[i]?cmnd  -- command from father
              IF
                cmnd='p'
                  IF
                    val=empty
                      up[i]!'p';0  --reply end of print
                    TRUE
                      down[lchild]!'p' -- left subtree
                cmnd='i'
                  SEQ
                    down[i]?v
                    IF
                      val=empty  -- empty node
                        SEQ
                          val=v -- store value
                          up[i]!iackpos;v -- pos reply
                      v<val  -- search left subtree
                        SEQ
                          down[lchild]!'i';v
                      TRUE     -- search right subtree
                        SEQ
                          down[rchild]!'i';v
                cmnd='c'      -- check command
                  SEQ
                    down[i]?v
                    IF
                      val=empty  -- node empty
                        up[i]!cackneg;v -- neg reply
                      val=v
                        up[i]!cackpos;v -- pos reply
                      v<val  -- search left subtree
                        SEQ
                          down[lchild]!'c';v
                      TRUE     -- search right subtree
                        SEQ
                          down[rchild]!'c';v
            up[left]?ans  -- answer from left child
              SEQ
                up[left]?val
                IF
                  ans='p' -- if token reply
                    SEQ
                      up[i]!0;val  -- send value
                      down[right]!'p'-- and token right
                  TRUE
                    up[i]!ans;val  -- else send reply
            up[right]?ans  -- ans from right child
              SEQ
```

Continued

Continued

```
                up[right]?val
                up[i]!ans;val   -- send reply to father


--
-- interface process
--
--
VAR ans,val,checkallowed,printallowed,insertallowed :
SEQ
  checkallowed := TRUE
  printallowed := TRUE
  insertallowed := TRUE
  ALT
    ALT i=[0 FOR n]
      insertallowed & ini[i]?ANY
        -- set checkallowed and printallowed to FALSE
        -- send command to root of tree
      checkallowed & inc[i]?ANY
        -- set insertallowed to be FALSE
        -- send command to root of tree
      printallowed & inp[i]?ANY
        --set printallowed and insertallowed to FALSE
        -- send command to root of tree
    ALT
      intree?reply
        -- update insertallowed,printallowed and
        -- checkallowed as necessary
        -- send reply to client
```

Fig. 8.6 occam code for concurrent access to binary tree.

The occam code for these operations on a binary tree structure, as shown in Fig. 8.5, is shown in Fig. 8.6.

The interface process now may receive inputs from both the clients and the root node of the tree concurrently but must process them sequentially and hence must use an ALT construct. It must only accept requests from clients, however, if the synchronization constraints allow. It is not possible to do this using a single channel from client to interface since all types of requests would be blocked if the current type of request could not be accepted. Hence we need three different channels, one for each operation type. The example shows three different channels per client to the interface process, although similar client channels could be multiplexed into a single one to the interface process, since the synchronization requirements are based on request type, not client identity. Note also that in this solution the replies have to be tagged with the command they are responding to since replies may be ordered differently to requests. Although not shown, replies actually need more information than just the command they are responding to; they need to know which client generated the request so that the reply can be routed to the appropriate one. The solution to this is one of those discussed in the distributed processes chapter. Note also that this solution does not check for overflow; specifically whether an insert will go too far down one branch of the tree.

In addition to this relatively large scale concurrency there is also a possibility of using some smaller scale concurrency within the operations in the nodes. For example, in the printing operation all the values of the descendants of a node are required, but in a particular order. Instead of requesting them in sequential order they could be requested in parallel but only accepted in the required sequential order. This is only sensible if the tree becomes large and the communication costs relatively high. We give the solution using this form of low-level concurrency in Fig. 8.7.

In this solution we have had to add some extra channels to each node called **pup**, which carry replies from each node to its parent for the print command only. This is because each node can only receive replies from its children to a print command in a particular order, left children first and then right children. We implement this by means of a Boolean condition in the guards for the appropriate channels. However, since we may process requests concurrently replies from checking may always be received from the right child while those from the print command may not. The only simple way to differentiate between the replies is to use a separate channel for the replies to different commands. The complications introduced for this concurrency-in-the-small do not seem worthwhile in this case and would probably not be used in a real implementation.

8.2 BALANCING THE TREE

The time taken to access items in a binary tree structure depends on the number of nodes to be traversed to find the items. This depends on the structure of the tree. A balanced tree where the level of any branch is no more than one greater or lesser than the level of any other branch is the most efficient and a number of algorithms have been developed to balance a tree structure. The standard sequential algorithm (Tremblay and Sorenson, 1984) for balancing a tree involves searching for unbalanced nodes and then balancing them by rearranging the structure of the subtrees involved using pointer manipulation. We cannot do this pointer manipulation on our static structure of a tree of processes since the channels which are equivalent to the pointers of a standard tree structure are static. The arrangement of channels which is equivalent to pointers is total connection, since a pointer value can be changed to point to any other node. Assuming that we set up a total connection structure between the node, then we could map any binary tree structure on to this by using the appropriate channels. In this regime we could balance the tree using the same algorithms as the sequential case.

In the example below link is a vector of channels which provides two

```
DEF empty = ...   -- initial value held in nodes
DEF n = ... :  -- maximum number of nodes
CHAN down[n],up[n],pup[n] :
PAR
  PAR i=[0 FOR n]
    DEF lchild = (2*i) + 1 :  -- left index
    DEF rchild = lchild + 1 : -- right index
    VAR val,rallow :
    SEQ
      rallow := FALSE -- disallow print from r subtree
      val := empty
      WHILE TRUE
        VAR v,ans,cmnd :
        SEQ
          ALT
            down[i]?cmnd
              IF
                cmnd='p'
                  IF
                    val=empty  -- node empty
                      pup[i]!'p' -- reply token
                    TRUE
                      PAR
                        down[lchild]!'p'--send left
                        down[rchild]!'p'--and right
                cmnd='i'
                  SEQ
                    down[i]?v
                    IF
                      val=empty
                        SEQ
                          val=v
                          up[i]!iackpos;v -- pos ack
                      v<val
                        down[lchild]!'i';v -- send left
                      TRUE
                        down[rchild]!'i';v --send right
                cmnd='c'
                  SEQ
                    down[i]?v
                    IF
                      val=empty
                        up[i]!cackneg;v -- neg ack
                      val=v
                        up[i]!cackpos;v -- pos ack
                      v<val
                        SEQ
                          down[lchild]!'c';v -- left
                      TRUE
                        SEQ
                          down[rchild]!'c';v -- right


            up[lchild]?ans
              SEQ
                up[lchild]?val
                up[i]!ans;val -- send reply to father
            up[rchild]?ans
              SEQ
                up[rchild]?val
                up[i]!ans;val -- reply to father
            pup[lchild]?ans
              IF
                ans='p'
                  SEQ
                    pup[i]!val -- send token
                    rallow := TRUE -- allow right inp
                  TRUE
```

```
                    pup[i]!ans
            rallow & pup[rchild]?ans
              SEQ
                IF
                  ans='p'
                    rallow := FALSE -- stop right inp
                  TRUE
                    SKIP
                pup[i]!ans -- reply to father


--
-- interface process
--
--
VAR ans,val,checkallowed,printallowed,insertallowed :
SEQ
  checkallowed := TRUE
  printallowed := TRUE
  insertallowed := TRUE
  ALT
    ALT i=[0 FOR n]
      insertallowed & ini[i]?ANY
        -- set checkallowed and printallowed to FALSE
        -- send command to root of tree
      checkallowed & inc[i]?ANY
        -- set insertallowed to be FALSE
        -- send command to root of tree
      printallowed & inp[i]?ANY
        --set printallowed and insertallowed to FALSE
        -- send command to root of tree
    ALT
      intree?reply
        -- update insertallowed,printallowed and
        -- checkallowed as necessary
        -- send reply to client
```

Fig. 8.7 Code for binary tree with more concurrency.

way communication between every pair of nodes. One node, node 0, is designated the interface node which implements the synchronization and communicates with the clients as before. The links between a pair of nodes i and j, are given by:

link[i*n+j] for the link from i to j
link[j*n+i] for the link from j to i

The transformations required to balance a tree are one of the four cases shown below (Tremblay and Sorenson, 1984). In each case the transformation requires some of the links of the present tree to be changed to point to a different subtree. Considering a simple example, the tree shown on the left in Fig. 8.8 is equivalent to the one on the right on the assumption that, for any node, its right subchild contains a value less than itself and its left subchild contains a value greater than itself. For example, the standard tree walk algorithms would give an identical sequence for the two trees. The relationship between these two trees is expressed in general form by the transformation in Fig. 8.9.

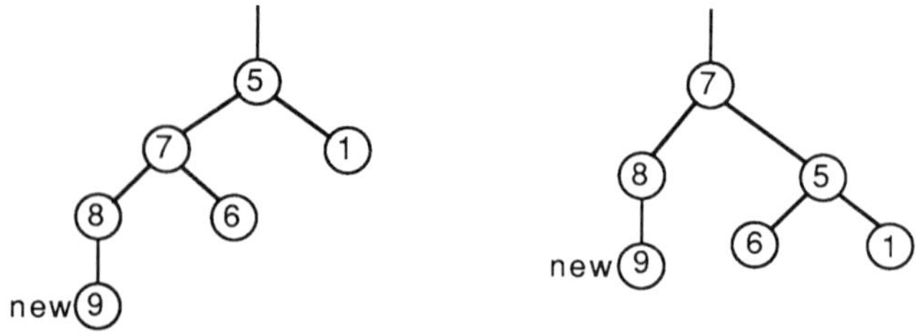

Fig. 8.8 Balancing a tree.

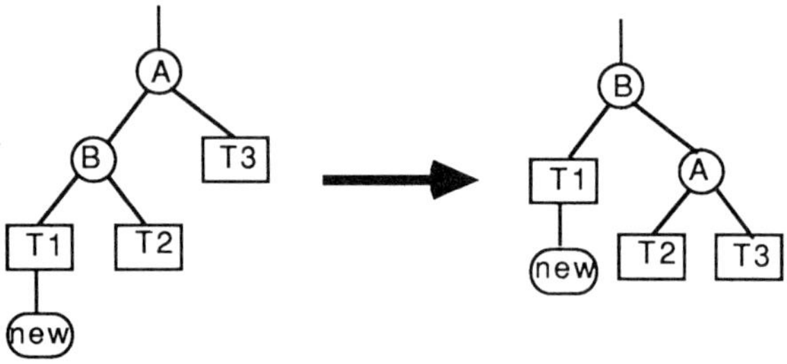

Fig. 8.9 Tree transformation 1.

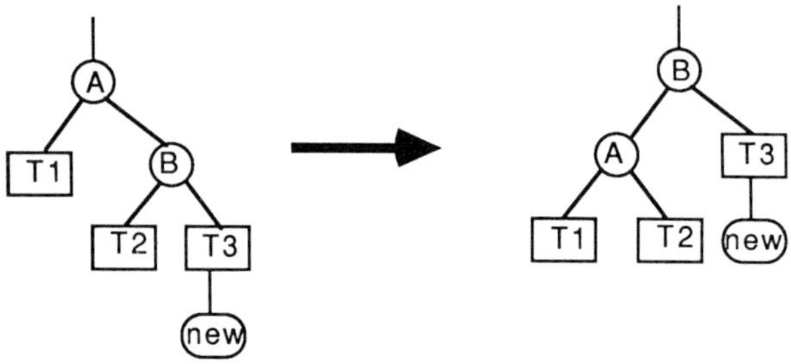

Fig. 8.10 Tree transformation 2.

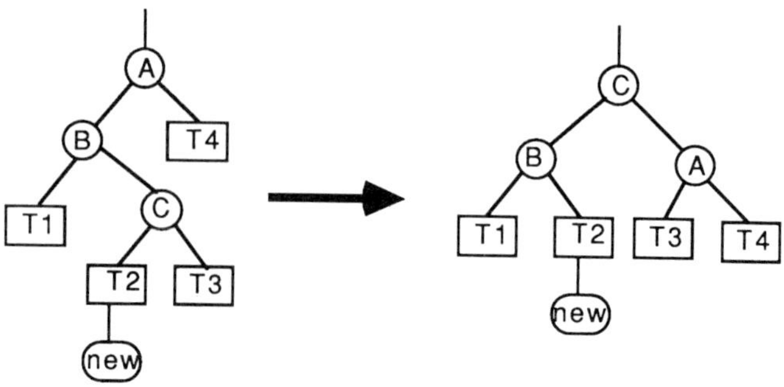

Fig. 8.11 Tree transformation 3.

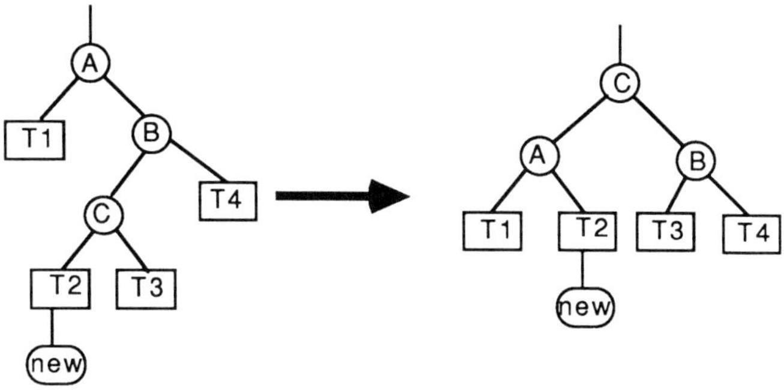

Fig. 8.12 Tree transformation 4.

The code for this solution is given in Fig. 8.13.

```
DEF empty = ... : -- initial node value
DEF n = ... :  -- maximum number of nodes
DEF nxn = n*n :  -- total connection
DEF insert = ..., -- code for insert command
    print = ..., -- code for print command
    check = ..., -- code for check command
    pend = ..., -- code for end of printing data
    nclients = ..., -- no. of client processes
    iack = ..., -- code for insert acknowledgement
    cack = ..., -- code for check acknowledgement
    pack = ..., -- code for print acknowledgement
    ackpos = ..., -- code for positive acknowledgement
    ackneg = ..., -- code for negative acknowledgement
    allnodesused = ...: -- code for out of node storage
DEF m1 = ..., -- codes for rebalancing -- node B case 1
    m2 = ..., -- node B case 3
    m3 = ..., -- node B case 2
    m4 = ..., -- node B case 4
    m5 = ..., -- node C case 3
    m6 = ...: -- node C case 4
CHAN link[nxn] : -- total connection both ways
CHAN connection[n],free[n],alloc[n] :
                   --  channels to channel and node manager
PAR
  PAR i=[1 FOR n-1] -- nodes except interface
    VAR parent,rchild,lchild,rplength,lplength,cmnd,
        val,v,bi,temp1,temp,ralloc,lalloc,cchan,ack :
    SEQ
      val := empty  -- initially node is empty
      free[i]!ANY   -- message to node manager
      connection[i]?parent  -- find out who parent is
      rchild := empty
      ralloc := FALSE  -- no children at present
      lchild := empty
      lalloc := FALSE
      lplength := 0  -- initial path length from left child
      rplength := 0  -- initial path length from right child
      WHILE TRUE
        ALT
          link[(parent*n) + i]?cmnd -- command from parent
            IF
              cmnd=insert  -- insert command
                SEQ
```

Continued

```
          link[(parent*n) + i]?v  -- insert value
          IF
            val=empty
              SEQ
                val := v
                link[(i*n) + parent]!iack;0;'B'
                -- reply path length and balanced
            v<val  -- go left
              SEQ
                IF
                  lchild=empty  -- get new link
                    SEQ
                      alloc[i]!ANY  -- get free node
                      connection[i]?lchild
                      lalloc := TRUE
                  TRUE
                    SKIP
                IF
                  lchild<>allnodesused  -- free node
                    link[(i*n) + lchild]!insert;v
                  TRUE  --  no free nodes
                    link[(i*n)+parent]!iack;
                      allnodesused;'B'
            TRUE  -- go right and same action as above
              SEQ
                IF
                  rchild=empty
                    SEQ
                      alloc[i]!ANY
                      connection[i]?rchild
                      ralloc := TRUE
                  TRUE
                    SKIP
                IF
                  rchild<>allnodesused
                    link[(i*n)+rchild]!insert;v
                  TRUE
                    link[(i*n)+parent]!iack;
                      allnodesused;'B'
      cmnd=m1  -- node B position case 1 in rebalancing
        SEQ  -- relink as diagram of case 1
          link[(parent*n)+i]?temp
          rplength := lplength
          link[(i*n)+parent]!rchild
          rchild := parent
          parent := temp
          link[(i*n)+parent]!rplength;'B'
      cmnd=m2  -- node B case 3 relinking
        SEQ
          link[(parent*n)+i]?temp
          link[(i*n)+parent]!rchild
          link[(i*n)+rchild]!m5;temp;parent
          link[(rchild*n)+i]?temp
          parent := rchild
          rchild := temp
          rplength := lplength
      cmnd=m5  -- node C position case 3 relinking
        SEQ
          link[(parent*n)+i]?temp1;temp
          link[(i*n)+parent]!lchild
          parent := temp1
          link[(i*n)+temp]!rchild
          rchild := temp
          lplength := lplength + 1
          rplength := lplength
          link[(i*n)+parent]!lplength;'B'
```

```
    cmnd=m3  -- node B position case 2 relinking
      SEQ
        link[(parent*n)+i]?temp
        lplength := rplength
        link[(i*n)+parent]!lchild
        lchild := parent
        parent := temp
        link[(i*n)+parent]!lplength;'B'
    cmnd=m4  -- node B position case 4 relinking
      SEQ
        link[(parent*n)+i]?temp
        link[(i*n)+parent]!lchild
        link[(i*n)+lchild]!m6;temp;parent
        link[(lchild*n)+i]?temp
        parent := lchild
        lchild := temp
        lplength := rplength
    cmnd=m6  -- node C position case 4 relinking
      SEQ
        link[(parent*n)+i]?temp1;temp
        link[(i*n)+parent]!rchild
        parent := temp1
        link[(i*n)+temp]!lchild
        lchild := temp
        rplength := rplength + 1
        lplength := rplength
        link[(i*n)+parent]!rplength;'B'
    cmnd=check  -- check command from parent
      SEQ
        link[(parent*n)+i]?v;cchan -- value to check
        IF
          val=empty  -- negative result
            link[(i*n)+parent]!cack;ackneg;v;cchan
          val=v  -- positive result
            link[(i*n)+parent]!cack;ackpos;v;cchan
          val<v  -- go down tree left
            SEQ
              IF
                link[(i*n)+lchild]=empty
                  link[(i*n)+parent]!cack;ackneg;v;cchan
                TRUE
                  link[(i*n)+lchild]!check;v;cchan
          TRUE  -- go down tree right
            SEQ
              IF
                link[(i*n)+rchild]=empty
                  link[(i*n)+parent]!cack;ackneg;v;cchan
                TRUE
                  link[(i*n)+rchild]!check;v;cchan
    cmnd=print  -- print command from parent
      IF
        link[(i*n)+lchild]=empty  -- go left if possible
          SEQ
            link[(i*n)+parent]!pack;val
            IF
              link[(i*n)+rchild]=empty
                link[(i*n)+parent]!print
              TRUE
                link[(i*n)+rchild]!print
        TRUE
          link[(i*n)+lchild]!print
lalloc & link[(lchild*n)+i]?cmnd --reply from left child
  IF
    cmnd=iack  -- ack of insert command
      SEQ
        link[(lchild*n) + i]?lplength;bi
```

Continued

Continued

```
        IF
          (lplength-rplength)=2 -- rebalancing reqd?
            SEQ
              IF
                bi='L'  -- yes
                  SEQ
                    link[(i*n)+lchild]!m1;parent
                    -- new parent node for lchild
                    link[(lchild*n)+i]?temp
                    parent := lchild
                    lchild := temp
                    lplength := rplength
                TRUE  -- yes
                  SEQ
                    link[(i*n)+lchild]!m2;parent
                    -- req node no of left child
                    -- and send parents id
                    link[(lchild*n)+i]?parent
                    link[(parent*n)+i]?lchild
                    lplength := rplength-1
          TRUE -- no
            SEQ
              lplength := lplength + 1
              IF
                lplength>rplength
                  link[(i*n)+parent]!iack;lplength;'L'
                lplength=rplength
                  link[(i*n)+parent]!iack;lplength;'B'
                TRUE
                  link[(i*n)+parent]!iack;rplength;'R'

    cmnd=cack -- ack of check command
      SEQ
        link[(lchild*n)+i]?ack;v;cchan
        link[(i*n)+parent]!cmnd;ack;v;cchan
    cmnd=print -- print token
      SEQ
        link[(i*n)+parent]!pack;val
        IF
          link[(i*n)+rchild]=empty
            link[(i*n)+parent]!print
          TRUE
            link[(i*n)+rchild]!print
    cmnd=pack -- print acknowledge
      SEQ
        link[(lchild*n)+i]?v
        link[(i*n)+parent]!pack;v
    TRUE
      SKIP
ralloc & link[(rchild*n)+i]?cmnd--reply from right child
  IF  -- code basically same as left child
    cmnd=iack
      SEQ
        link[(rchild*n)+i]?rplength;bi
        IF
          (rplength-lplength)=2
            SEQ
              IF
                bi='R'
                  SEQ
                    link[(i*n)+rchild]!m3;parent
                    link[(rchild*n)+i]?temp
                    parent := rchild
                    rchild := temp
                    rplength := lplength
                TRUE
```

```
                    SEQ
                      link[(i*n)+rchild]!m4;parent
                      link[(rchild*n)+i]?parent
                      link[(parent*n)+i]?rchild
                      rplength := lplength-1
            TRUE
              SEQ
                lplength := lplength + 1
                IF
                  lplength>rplength
                    link[(i*n)+parent]!iack;lplength;'L'
                  lplength=rplength
                    link[(i*n)+parent]!iack;lplength;'B'
                  TRUE
                    link[(i*n)+parent]!iack;rplength;'R'

      cmnd=cack
        SEQ
          link[(rchild*n)+i]?ack;v;cchan
          link[(i*n)+parent]!cmnd;ack;v;cchan
      cmnd=print
        link[(i*n)+parent]!print
      cmnd=pack
        SEQ
          link[(rchild*n)+i]?v
          link[(i*n)+parent]!pack;v
      TRUE
        SKIP
-- channel and node manager
VAR used :
SEQ -- scheduler
  used := 1  -- initially root used
  ALT i=[0 FOR n]
    alloc[i]?ANY
      SEQ
        IF
          used<>n
            ALT j=[1 FOR n-1]
              free[j]?ANY
                SEQ
                  connection[i]!j
                  connection[j]!i
          TRUE
            connection[i]!allnodesused

VAR clienti[nclient],clientir[nclient],clientp[nclient],
    clientpr[nclient],clientc[nclient],clientcr[nclient] :
PAR -- for interface and clients
  VAR root,v,temp,pending,insertprintallowed :
  SEQ
    insertprintallowed := TRUE
    root := empty
    WHILE TRUE  -- remember separate channels for diff commands
      ALT
        ALT i=[0 FOR nclients]
          ALT
            insertprintallowed & clienti[i]?v -- insert command
              SEQ
                insertprintallowed := FALSE
                IF
                  root=empty
                    SEQ
                      alloc[0]!ANY -- get free node
                      connection[0]?temp
                      IF
```

Continued

Continued

```
                    temp<>allnodesused
                      SEQ
                        link[temp]!insert;v
                        root := temp
                        pending := i
                    TRUE
                      SEQ
                        clientir[i]!fail
                        insertprintallowed := TRUE
              TRUE
                link[root]!insert;v
        insertprintallowed & clientp[i]?ANY -- print request
          IF
            root=empty
              clientpr[i]!pend
            TRUE
              SEQ
                link[root]!print
                pending := i
                insertprintallowed := FALSE
        clientc[i]?v  -- check request
          IF
            root=empty
              clientcr[i]!ackneg;v
            TRUE
              link[root]!check;v;i
    link[root*n]?reply  -- reply from tree
      IF
        reply=iack  -- insert acknowledge
          SEQ
            link[root*n]?lplength;bi
            IF
              lplength=allnodesused
                clientir[pending]!ackneg
              TRUE
                clientir[pending]!ackpos
            insertprintallowed := TRUE
        reply=cack  -- check acknowledge
          SEQ
            link[root*n]?ack;v;cl
            clientcr[cl]!ack;v
        reply=pack  -- print acknowledge
          SEQ
            link[root*n]?v
            clientpr[pending]!v
            IF
              v=print
                SEQ
                  insertprintallowed := TRUE
              TRUE
                SKIP
```

Fig. 8.13 occam code for concurrent access to binary tree including rebalancing.

In the standard sequential algorithm, after insertion the branch of the tree which has just had the insertion made is searched in an upwards direction, checking each node from the leaf to the root node. Whenever a critical node is discovered the subtrees beneath are rebalanced using one of four standard transformations. Since the nodes are autonomous in our solution the algorithm has to be implemented on each node with message passing between nodes denoting the balancing actions required. The transformations involve changing the connections between nodes which, in our model, implies changing the links which are used for a node to communicate with its parent, right child and left child. Since rebalancing could occur anywhere on the path between a leaf and the root multiple insertions should not be allowed concurrently since this could produce multiple interleaved balancing actions which could corrupt the tree structure. The required synchronization is implemented in the interface process as before.

Using a balanced representation such as the one in Fig. 8.13 balancing on insertion is not really feasible since it requires moving data about in complicated patterns. If it was really necessary it would probably be better to output the tree into a vector and insert it again to form a balanced tree by choosing the inputs in the correct order. This is left as an exercise for the reader (Exercise 8.2).

In this solution to the balancing problem we have implicitly assumed that the cost of moving data is high compared to the cost of rearranging the links. If this assumption is incorrect, or if the tree structure is fixed, for example, because it is a hardware rather than a software architecture, then it may be more appropriate or necessary to move data between nodes rather than to change the links to balance the tree. In this case balancing occurs on insertion of data and follows the same transformations as given previously. The code for this solution becomes quite complex since data has to be moved about in complex patterns around the tree but the solution follows the general pattern of the last program, that is, a process represents a node and responds to commands by sending replies.

SUMMARY Chapter 8

In this chapter the representation of data structures as collections of processes has been investigated. This type of representation makes it possible to introduce concurrency into the accessing of data structures. However, the introduction of more and more concurrency complicates the model since more information has to be carried around within the structure and more complicated synchronization constraints have to be implemented. The question of how much concurrency is required in a data structure can only be answered by reference to the particular problem to be solved since this will dictate the frequency of access, the operations required and the speed of response necessary.

EXERCISES Chapter 8

E8.1 Modify the occam code for the insertion operation given in Fig. 8.3 to include checks for storage overflow. Does this require alterations to the code for the check and print operations also?

E8.2 Modify the occam code of Fig. 8.3 so that if storage overflow occurs on insertion balancing of the tree is attempted. (Hint: output the values to a vector in the root node and reinsert them.)

E8.3 What are the advantages and disadvantages of representing the tree as a static set of totally connected nodes with the required structure mapped on to this and representing the tree as a set of nodes linked only in the required structure with a pool of unused nodes?

E8.4 Implement the occam code necessary to balance a tree on insertion by moving the data rather than changing the links.

9

SIMULATION OF AN OPERATING SYSTEM

To show the use of some of the techniques we have illustrated in previous chapters we consider here the design of a program which resembles an operating system in miniature. We give the code for most of the system in occam although for the sake of brevity we omit some details. Our concern is with the logical design of the system rather than with the physical implementation and thus we ignore many features which would be of interest in a real system, such as, for example, the allocation scheme for blocks on a disc. Also, to keep the problem to a manageable size, we have limited ourselves to a small number of commands.

9.1 THE PROBLEM

A computer system comprises of the following set of resources:

a n.r readers which are input devices only,
b n.p printers which are output devices only,
c n.d disc drives which are input–output devices and store sets of files, and
d a single control terminal.

A user sits at the control terminal and issues commands to the system. The commands available are:

a R reader file
read information from the specified reader and store it as the specified file.
b P file
print the contents of the specified file on any available printer.

c L reader
   print the information from the specified reader on any available printer.

d E file
   erase the specified file.

for example,

R 1 data

means read information from reader 1 and store it in a file called data.

The objective of the operating system is to control the use of resources and to allow as much concurrency of operation as possible, for example, a command to input from a reader to a file should be performed concurrently with an operation to print the input from a different reader. Thus the set of requested operations should be performed in the minimum elapsed time.

9.2 DESIGN

From the discussion of the problem given above it is obvious that the operating system has to control the operation of the resources, taking its commands as the sequence of input from the control terminal. The simplest way to model this is to associate a process with each device.This process controls the device and accepts commands for it and send replies from it to the operating system process. This leads to an outline structure as shown in Fig. 9.1.

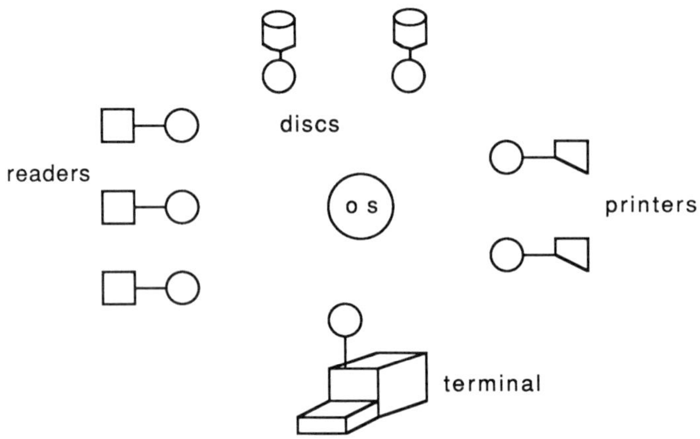

Fig. 9.1 Outline structure of problem.

The channel connections required in such a system are, bearing in mind the commands available,

- **a** between the operating system process and all the other processes in both directions to carry commands from the operating system to the device processes and status information from the device processes to the operating system,
- **b** from every reader processes to every disc and printer process to carry data in response to R and L commands,
- **c** from every disc process to every printer process to carry data in response to P commands.

The reason for the asymmetry here is that the readers are explicitly addressed in the commands whilst printers are anonymous, that is, they are all identical and any free one may be used in an operation. Thus a reader is addressed explicitly whilst a printer is selected for use via a scheduler, that is, all processes which may send data to a printer are totally connected to all printers and the channel to be used for any print transaction is given by the scheduler; the cross-bar switch solution of Chapter 5.

Turning our attention to the disc sub-system, we see that a disc contains a set of files. We shall assume, conventionally, that files are accessed via a directory which converts file names to disc addresses. There are two options for the directory organization; we could have a directory for each individual disc or a single directory for the complete sub-system. We adopt the former solution here since this gives more possibilities for concurrency. Access to a file therefore involves an access to the directory and an access to the disc store. To obtain concurrency we separate the directory and disc store into two communicating processes. We shall now refer to the devices and the directory as resources and it is the operating system which is responsible for scheduling the use of these resources via commands to their associated processes.

9.2.1 An outline design

If we first consider a sequential implementation we see that the operating system process continually reads a command from the terminal, signals the appropriate resources to perform the operation and waits for replies from the resource processes indicating the completion of the command. Assuming, as is normally the case in practice, that data transfer takes considerably longer than the operation set-up, the operating system process will be idle for a considerable period of time between issuing commands and receiving completion replies. Also resources not involved in the execution of that command will be idle.

An alternative approach, potentially involving more concurrency and hence higher throughput, is to allow the operating system to read the next command whilst the present one is being processed and to execute the second command concurrently with the first if the required resources are available. This approach can be extended to allow the execution of many commands concurrently. In order for the operating system to know which resources are available it must keep track of which ones have been allocated to command execution and which ones are free and it must do this by means of asynchronous processes since the timing of resource free replies cannot be known in advance. Before launching a new command the operating system has to check for the availability of the necessary resources. If the required resources are not available then the operating system idles until they become available.

Consecutive commands involving at least one common resource will cause the commands to be executed sequentially, thus reducing concurrency. One solution to this is to internally buffer any commands which cannot be executed immediately due to the unavailability of some resources. Using this technique, commands from the user will not necessarily be executed in the order presented. This may cause problems due to dependencies such as the one given below.

```
R 1 X -- create file X and fill with data from reader 1
P X   -- print the contents of file X on any available printer
```

If a previous command is still using reader 1 then the read operation above cannot be executed and will be buffered internally for later execution. However, under these circumstances the print command can be executed but execution would produce an error since the file X has not been created yet. Thus to be able to execute commands out of order the operating system must first discover whether there are any data dependencies between the candidate command and any commands delayed in the internal buffer. This is posed as a problem in the exercises at the end of this chapter.

To obtain more concurrency it would be possible to change the connection between the operating system and the resource processes to include buffering, either by including buffers or by including extra courier processes. This would overcome the problem of ordering since commands would still be executed in the correct order but would still suffer from the problem of idle processes if consecutive commands required the same resource. Even if the problem of data dependency between commands is left to the operating system there seems to be little advantage in this solution if, as we postulated previously, data transfer takes considerably longer than control set-up.

We have chosen to implement the solution where commands may be executed out of sequence although we have deliberately omitted some of the details and left them as exercises for the reader.

9.2.2 Design of the individual resource processes

Considering the design of a reader process first we see that this process has interfaces to the operating system process, the disk store processes, the associated reader and the printer processes. Each reader process has two channels to the operating system process, one to receive commands and one to inform the operating system when the device is free. Each reader process is also connected to each printer process and also to the printer scheduler to request a printer connection and to receive the allocated channel reply. Since a command is available to store input in a file the readers are connected unidirectionally to each disc storage process. The allocation of files to discs is an operating system policy and hence the scheduling is performed by the operating system rather than a separate scheduler. Hence the channel to use in reader to disc operations is provided by the operating system process (Fig. 9.2).

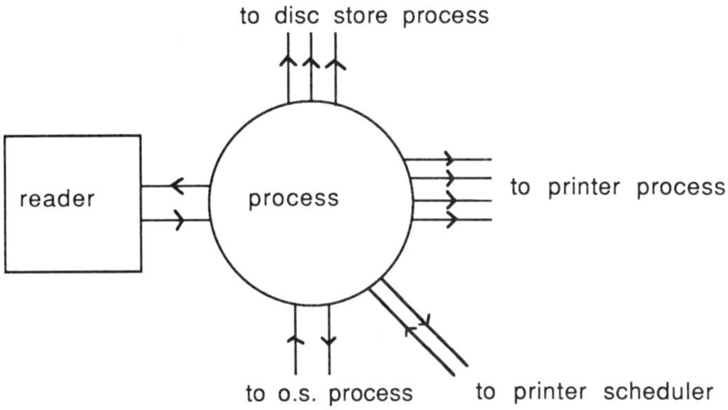

Fig. 9.2 Reader interface.

Considering the design of a printer sub-system next we see that this is virtually identical to the crossbar switch solution of Chapter 5, except that the inputs are from two different sources, the disc store process and the reader processes.

The design of a disc sub-system is slightly different in that two processes are involved, a directory process and a storage process for each disc. The directory process is connected to the operating system process bidirectionally to receive commands and send replies. It is also connected to its associated disc storage process to send and receive addresses of files. The disc storage processes are connected to every reader process for input, to every printer process for output, to the printer scheduler for request and allocation of a printer channel, to the associated directory

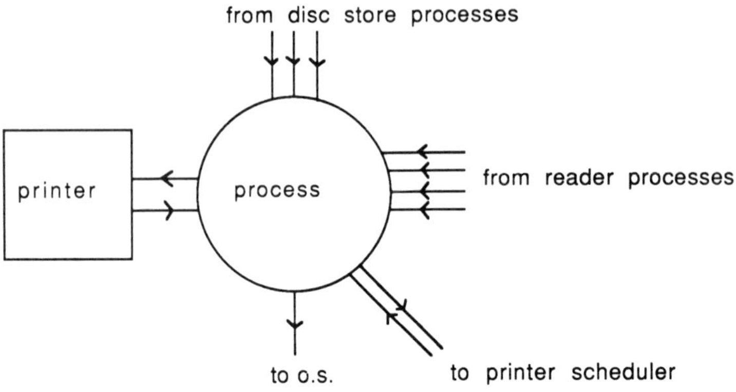

Fig. 9.3 Printer interface.

process for receiving and sending disc storage addresses and to the operating system to receive commands and send replies (Fig. 9.4).

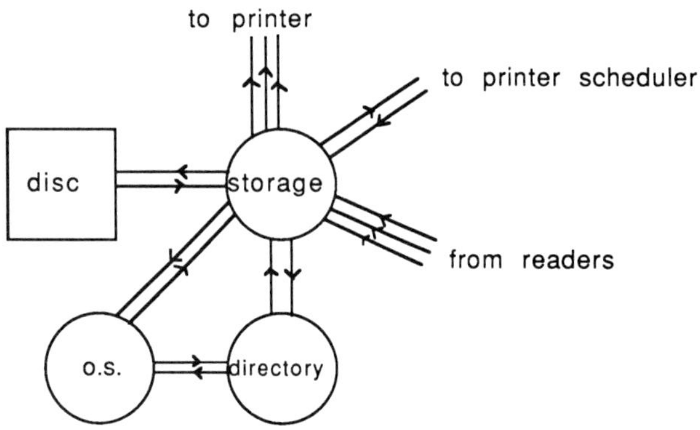

Fig. 9.4 Disc interface

The terminal process is very simple since it only receives input from the terminal, edits it and performs input validation. The command and its parameters are passed to the operating system process (Fig. 9.5).

The operating system process is the most complex since it has to send

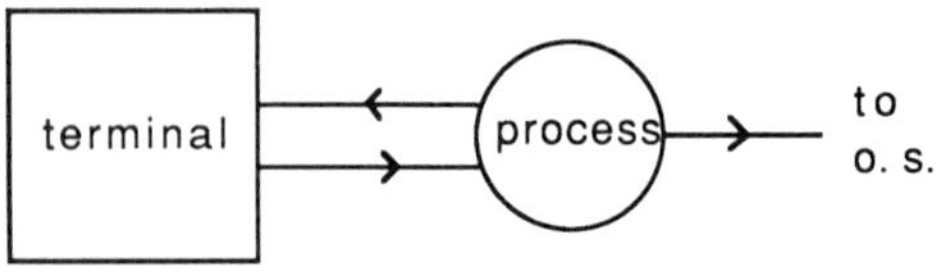

Fig. 9.5 Terminal interface.

the appropriate commands to the other processes, allowing as much concurrency as possible. Since synchronous communication will block the sender if the receiver is not ready, the operating system should not send commands to processes which are not ready to receive them otherwise it will be blocked and not able to issue other commands. Therefore the operating system has to keep track of the resources in use and those available, which it does by means of a table of flags for the readers and discs and a count for the printers since they are anonymous. In order to obtain as much concurrency as possible the operating system may have to obey commands out of order if some resources are in use. This implies that the operating system has to keep an internal queue of waiting commands which were blocked when first requested and that these waiting commands have to be periodically reawakened to see if they can then be run. Complex scheduling strategies could be used here to determine which command is selected at any time but here we use a simple strategy of choosing those in the queue before new commands from the terminal. In order for the operating system to keep track of resource utilization, resources have to signal when they become free. This could be done on a per command basis, but, because of the asynchronism of the processes, it is much easier to perform this on a per resource basis. Hence in our design each resource signals to the operating system when it has finished its current action.

The actions taken by the operating system are therefore to accept replies freeing resources and noting them, between accepting commands from the internal queue, which has priority, and the terminal. In order to see whether the command can be executed the operating system checks its internal tables to see if the required resources are free. If so the command is activated by sending commands to the appropriate resource processes, otherwise the command is stored in the internal queue and another command selected (Figs 9.6 and 9.7).

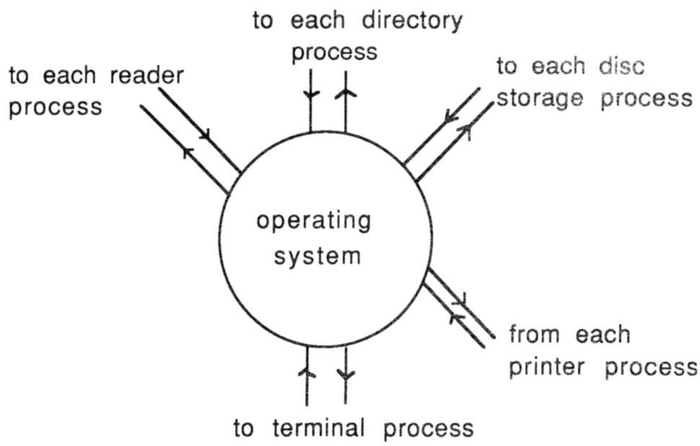

Fig. 9.6 Operating system interface.

```
CHAN readerreply[n.r],ostoreader[n.r],readertoscheduler[n.r],
     schedulertoreader[n.r],
     printertoscheduler[n.p],schedulertoprinter[n.p],
     printerreply[n.p],
     discreply[n.d],ostodisc[n.d],disctoscheduler[n.d],
     schedulertodisc[n.d],ostodirectory[n.d],directorytoos[n.d],
     directorytodisc[n.d],disctodirectory[n.d] :

 -- reader process

PROC readerprocess(VALUE i)=

  PROC outtodisc=
  -- code for sending stream to disc
  :

  PROC outtoprinter=
  -- code for sending stream to printer
  :

  WHILE TRUE
    VAR cmnd,param1,ch :
    SEQ
      readerreply[i]!ANY  -- signal reader free
      ostoreader[i]?cmnd  -- wait for command
      IF
        cmnd='R'          -- R command
          SEQ
            ostoreader[i]?ch  -- send to disc param1
            ch:=((i*n.d)+ch)
            outtodisc     --send stream to appropriate channel
        cmnd='L'          -- T command
          SEQ
            readertoscheduler[i]!ANY -- request printer channel
            schedulertoreader[i]?ch   -- get printer channel
            outtoprinter             -- send stream to printer
        TRUE
          SKIP :

  -- printer processes

PROC printerprocess(VALUE i)=

  PROC receive=
  -- code to receive stream from disc or reader
  :

  WHILE TRUE
    VAR ch :
    SEQ
      printertoscheduler[i]!ANY  -- signal free
      schedulertoprinter[i]?ch   -- receive allocated channel
      receive
      printerreply[i]!ANY :      -- tell os resource free

PROC printerscheduler=

  -- connection process

  PROC conn(VALUE i,j,x,source)=
    VAR z :
    SEQ
      IF
        source='R'
          SEQ
            z:=(i*n.r)+j
            schedulertoreader[j]!z
            schedulertoprinter[i]!z
```

```
        TRUE
          SEQ
            z:=((i+n.r)*x)+j
            schedulertodisc[j]!z
            schedulertoprinter[i]!z  :

  WHILE TRUE
    ALT
      ALT j=[0 FOR n.p]
        printertoscheduler[j]?ANY
          ALT
            ALT i=[0 FOR n.r]
              readertoscheduler[i]?ANY
                conn(j,i,n.r,'R')
            ALT i=[0 FOR n.d]
              disctoscheduler[j]?ANY
                conn(j,i,n.d,'D') :

  -- directory process
PROC directoryprocess(VALUE i)=

  PROC boolsearch=
    -- code to search directory for param and return TRUE or FALSE
    :


  PROC positionsearch=
    -- return position of param in directory in addr
    :

  PROC makeentry=
    -- enter new name(param) and disc address(addr) in directory
    :
  PROC delete=
    -- delete param from directory


  VAR cmnd,param,result,addr:
  SEQ
     -- initialise directory here
     WHILE TRUE
       SEQ
         ostodirectory[i]?cmnd;param
         IF
           cmnd='E'
              delete
           cmnd='R'
             SEQ
               boolsearch
               directorytoos[i]!result
           cmnd='P'
             SEQ
               positionsearch
               directorytodisc[i]!addr
           cmnd='W'
             SEQ
               disctodirectory[i]?addr
               makeentry
           TRUE
             SKIP :

   -- disc process
 PROC discprocess(VALUE i)=

   PROC outfile=
```

Continued

Continued

```
          -- send stream to printer
          :

        PROC readfromreader=
          -- receive stream of chars from reader
          :
        WHILE TRUE
          VAR cmnd,ch,param,discaddr  :
          SEQ
            discreply[i]!ANY
            ostodisc[i]?cmnd
            IF
              cmnd='P'
                SEQ
                  directorytodisc[i]?discaddr
                  disctoscheduler[i]!ANY
                  schedulertodisc[i]?ch
                  outfile
              cmnd='R'
                SEQ
                  ostodisc[i]?param
                  ch:=i+(n.d*param)
                  readfromreader
                  disctodirectory[i]!discaddr
              TRUE
                SKIP :

        -- operating system process
      PROC osaction=

        PROC osprocess=
          VAR no,flag,found[n.d],use  :
          SEQ
            IF
              cmnd='E'
                PAR i=[0 FOR n.d]
                  ostodirectory[i]!'E';param1
              cmnd='L'
                IF
                  (reader[param1]=free) AND (printersinuse < n.p)
                    SEQ
                      ostoreader[param1]!'L'
                      reader[param1]:=busy
                      printersinuse:=printersinuse+1
                  TRUE
                    outqueue!'L';param1
              cmnd='P'
                SEQ
                  PAR i=[0 FOR n.d]
                    ostodirectory[i]!'R';param1
                    directorytoos[i]?found[i]
                  use:=-1
                  SEQ i=[0 FOR n.d]
                    IF
                      found[i]=TRUE
                        use:=i
                      TRUE
                        SKIP
                  IF
                    use=(-1)
                      outerr("file does not exist")
                    TRUE
                      IF
                        (disc[use]=free) AND (printersinuse<n.p)
                          SEQ
                            ostodisc[use]!'P'
```

```
                    ostodirectory[use]!'P';param1
                    disc[use]:=busy
                    printersinuse:=printersinuse+1
                TRUE
                  outqueue!'P';param1
        cmnd='R'
          SEQ
            IF
              reader[param1]=free
                SEQ
                  no:=0
                  flag:=TRUE
                  WHILE flag
                    IF
                      disc[no]=free
                        SEQ
                          ostoreader[param1]!'R';no
                          ostodirectory[no]!'w';param2
                          ostodisc[no]!'R';param1
                          reader[param1]:=busy
                          disc[no]:=busy
                          flag:=FALSE
                      TRUE
                        IF
                          no=n.d
                            SEQ
                              outqueue!'R';param1;param2
                              flag:=FALSE
                          TRUE
                            no:=no+1
              TRUE
                outqueue!'R';param1;param2
    TRUE
      SKIP :


VAR cmnd,param1,param2,printersinuse,reader[n.r],disc[n.d] :
SEQ
  printersinuse:=0
  WHILE TRUE
    PRI ALT
      ALT i=[0 FOR n.r]
        readerreply[i]?ANY
          reader[i]:=free
      ALT i=[0 FOR n.d]
        discreply[i]?ANY
          disc[i]:=free
      ALT i=[0 FOR n.p]
        printerreply[i]?ANY
          printersinuse:=printersinuse-1
      inqueue?cmnd;param1
        SEQ
          IF
            cmnd='R'
              inqueue?param2
            TRUE
              SKIP
          osprocess
      interminal?cmnd;param1
        SEQ
          IF
            cmnd='R'
              interminal?param2
            TRUE
```

Continued

Continued

```
                    SKIP
                osprocess :

  PAR
    PAR i=[0 FOR n.r]
      readerprocess(i)
    PAR i=[0 FOR n.p]
      printerprocess(i)
    PAR i=[0 FOR n.d]
      PAR
        directoryprocess(i)
        discprocess(i)
    printerscheduler
    osaction
    queue   -- process to queue delayed requests
    input   -- process to input commands and send to interminal
```

Fig. 9.7 Code for operating system.

We have deliberately left out some of the details of the data transfer between devices since they are simple and not relevant to the overall structure. We have also left out some other complications and left these as exercises for the interested reader.

The PRI ALT construct has been used in the code above. This construct is identical to an ALT construct except that if more than one guard evaluates to true the guarded process selected for execution is not chosen non-deterministically. Instead the process chosen for execution is the one whose guard evaluates to true and which occurs textually before the other processes whose guards evaluate to true. In effect each guarded process is given a priority dependent on its textual position in the PRI ALT and selection, when multiple guards evaluate to true, is dependent on the associated processes priority. The reason for its use here is to give replies freeing resources higher priority than requests for new resources. The use of the PRI ALT construct is explained in more detail in Chapter 10.

SUMMARY Chapter 9

This chapter has considered the problem of simulating an operating system in occam. The solution to this problem presented here shows some of the typical properties of occam programs, for example, the large number of channels involved in connecting processes together even when what seems to be the obvious functional decomposition is adopted. The solution also illustrates the use of some of the structures described earlier in this book.

At this point we should further consider the question of concurrency in this example. We have taken a particular level of decomposition in describing and implementing the solution presented here. We have justified the reason why we do not consider pipelining the commands to the resource processes as being that data transfer takes much longer than control set-up. In the particular instance given here we could have used the argument that the user cannot in general type in commands very fast and hence it is unlikely that much concurrency in command execution could actually be achieved unless the data transfer involved was very large. This is valid but we did not ignore this to introduce some extra concurrency. A question which arises is whether more concurrency could be obtained in the present problem. Since the way that concurrency in such a problem is obtained is by splitting the resources into finer grain we can see that the user sees the disc sub-system as a collection of files so we could also have made one of our resource categories files rather than discs and therefore potentially obtain more concurrency. It is interesting to see what the implications of this would have been. Since files have to be mapped on to discs the file processes have to contend for the use of the discs. Thus concurrency will be increased by having file processes but decreased by having to map them to discs. Furthermore more buffers will be required since buffers will presumably be allocated to file processes rather than disc processes. Since processes in occam are static we would have to allocate the maximum number of file processes at compile time, which would involve a considerable overhead of extra buffers. If we assume, as before, that data transfer takes considerably longer than control set-up there seems to be little gain in concurrency with this solution.

Thus the argument as to how much concurrency to build into the solution must depend on arguments as to how much time will be used in the various operations involved. As we have seen, assuming that data transfer is the overall time determining operation then there is little need to build in any more concurrency than our implemented solution. However, if the data transfer operation was not the time determining operation then we would have to reconsider the complete design and possibly introduce more concurrency.

EXERCISES Chapter 9

E9.1 The solution proposed in this chapter ignores the possibility that obeying commands out of sequence may invalidate them, for example, obeying the command to delete a file before a prior command to print the file has been executed. Modify the solution given to allow commands to be performed out of sequence only if the overall logic of the sequence is not affected.

E9.2 The code for the command queueing operation has not been included in the solution above. Suggest a solution bearing in mind that if there is any command in the queue it must be continually offered to the operating system process.

E9.3 The solution in this chapter ignores the possibility of errors, for example, asking to print a non-existent file, inputting into an already existing file and file storage overflow. Suggest modifications to deal with these and any other errors you can think of.

E9.4 Suggest modifications required to the operating system process to add the command:

C file1 file2

which copies the contents of file1 to file2, to the command repertoire.

E9.5 Assume that the data transfer operation takes approximately the same time as the control set-up. What changes would you make to the solution and why?

E9.6 Modify the solution given to take a file as the resource unit of data storage rather than a disc. How does this affect the concurrency of the solution?

E9.7 In this solution we used a crossbar switch to connect all the readers and discs to the printers. Would it have been better to have used couriers instead? If so, why?

10

CONCURRENCY, REAL TIME PROGRAMMING AND occam

In the examples we have considered so far time has only been important in that the reason for using concurrency has been to speed up the execution time of the program. However, there is a type of system called a real-time system which differs from other systems in that responses to external events must occur within a given time, that is, time is an important design criteria. In the design of real-time software it is the time constraints which are all important as we shall see in the examples given later.

10.1 REAL-TIME SYSTEMS

As an example of one type of real-time system, consider a customer using a cash dispenser at a bank. The computer controlling this terminal must respond quickly to a customer's request, otherwise he will become impatient and not use the terminal. Thus the only reason for requiring fast response is to satisfy the needs of the customer which, in terms of the timing required, is difficult to quantify and a wide range of response times would probably suffice. Consider, however, the computer employed in the control loop controlling an aircraft or controlling a nuclear power plant. Here the timing constraints are far more critical since failure to meet them may result in death. Also, in these cases, it is likely that the timing constraints can be specified far more precisely. Thus there is a wide range of real-time systems and the design of them will be different, with different priorities. We shall explore some of the properties of some simple systems later.

10.2 FACILITIES IN occam FOR REAL-TIME PROGRAMMING

Occam contains a number of facilities specifically to aid real-time programming. The simplest facility is a special form of channel called TIME which is connected to a clock which is updated at a constant, implementation defined rate. The channel TIME is special in that it may be used by multiple processes, unlike normal channels. However, a clock is local to a process, thus inputs from the channel TIME from different processes refer to different clocks and will not necessarily be related to one another. The value returned from reading the channel TIME is an unsigned integer and thus if two values are compared account must be taken of this since arithmetic in occam is performed in two's complement form. Clock values cycle between zero and a word consisting of a pattern of 1 bits. Thus simply subtracting two time values will not necessarily give the correct interval between them as an integer. Another trap for the unwary here is that the clock is incremented at an implementation dependent rate, which in many implementations, will be fast and hence the clock values will cycle quickly. If a user's process does not read the values sufficiently often it may miss one or more complete cycles of the clock thus invalidating any timing. As an example:

```
TIME ? curtime
```

will input the current value of the local clock into the variable curtime.

Another mechanism in occam for timing is a form of delay, thus the only effect of:

```
TIME ? AFTER x
```

is to cause execution of the issuing process to be delayed until the clock time is greater than the expression x. As we shall see in the examples later this form of delay is normally used after reading the clock value from the channel TIME and using this value with an increment as the delay time x.

A problem associated with timing is priority. If only one of a number of possible actions can be scheduled at a time how is the choice made? A standard scheduling method is to give the different actions different priorities depending on their importance and the scheduler simply chooses the pending action with the highest priority. This is how, for example, operating system processes get priority over user processes in a typical multi-user computer system. There are two situations in which this problem can arise in occam programs. Consider first the case of the execution of an ALT process where two or more of the guards evaluate to true. The rules of the language state that the process to execute in this case is one of the component processes whose guard has evaluated to true but that the actual process is chosen non-deterministically, that is, the programmer has no influence over the choice; it is chosen by the implementation. A problem arises if the implementation choice does not allow the user to meet real-time constraints. In this case he may wish to influence the order in which the implementation selects the process to execute. The PRI ALT process is provided in occam as an attempt to solve this problem. Use of this construct gives priorities to the component processes in textual order, that is, with the first component process having highest priority. When a PRI ALT is executed if two or more guards evaluate to true then the associated process with highest priority will be chosen for execution. One obvious use of this construct is to allow certain control signals to take precedence over the processing of data. For example, if a process wishes to accept data for processing over a channel and control signals over a separate channel then, if this is programmed using an ALT, there is no guarantee that if the process producing data produces data at a higher rate than this process consumes it that control signals will ever be received since the implementor of the system may have implemented the ALT so that the data input is always selected even if the control input is ready. Using a PRI ALT the control input can be given higher priority and hence will be selected in preference if both inputs are available. This can be extremely useful in dealing with special situations such as terminating data input and recovering from errors.

```
PRI ALT
  incntrl ? signal
    -- process signal
  indata ? data
    -- process data
```

There are a number of other situations, explained later, where this construction is useful.

The other situation where scheduling becomes important is where an occam program specifies that processes are to be run in PAR but the implementation is to be carried out on a system with less processors than the number of concurrent processes specified in the program. In this case several occam processes have to be multiplexed on to a single processor. PAR does not imply any particular ordering so the implementation may choose the order of executing the PAR processes. Just as in the case of ALT the user has no control over the ordering, which he may require for timing needs. A further problem here concerns the way in which the multiplexing of processes is implemented. On a transputer once a process is scheduled for execution it is not descheduled except at a few well characterized points. This again can cause timing problems as it can be difficult for the user to compute the time it will take to execute parts of his code which is a requirement is strict real-time constraints are to be met. In the same way that the use of PRI ALT gave priority to the constituent processes in textual order so the use of PRI PAR gives priority to the constituent processes of a PAR in textual order.

The reader should note that the imposition of priority via PRI ALT or PRI PAR has no effect on the logical operation of the program; the only effect is to change the order of scheduling processes for execution.

One other facility required for real-time programming in occam is some method of communication with the outside world. Occam communication is in the form of input and output over channels. We have seen that the method of communicating with a terminal is via the association of channels with particular devices. The same type of technique is used to communicate with real devices; a declaration associating a special channel with a device is included at the program.

```
CHAN DAC at 345 :
```

10.3 INTERRUPTS

The way in which sequential real-time programs are usually written is to code the input–output operations as interrupt driven routines which are activated in response to external events. The interrupt routines are kept as small as possible so that the response time to interrupts is small.

Occam does not have any mechanism akin to interrupts; there is no way of interrupting a process performing a computation to do something else. This is compensated to some extent by the presence of parallel processes since the programmer can code the input and output operations to occur in parallel with the computation processes. This has the advantage of removing the problems of shared data space which occur with interrupts since the occam model only allows communication via channels, all other values being local to the process in which they are declared. However, channel communication requires the computation process to listen at the appropriate time. This is polling and thus the computation process must poll the channels to the inputting processes at whatever rate is required by the system designer to meet the real-time constraints. In effect this comes down to saying that the computation process must look at the input–output channels after a certain number of instructions bearing in mind the speed of the underlying hardware.

10.4 DESIGNING REAL-TIME SYSTEMS

Before considering some examples let us consider, briefly, how we can meet real-time constraints. A typical real-time program will have an input and output process which is in a loop continually processing input and output. The input and output values will be communicated to other processes in the system via channels. In order to meet the real-time constraints imposed by the problem the designer has to calculate various times, such as the worst case time between the system responding to its inputs and the worst case time required to propagate the effect of an input to an output. In order to do this he has to calculate the time taken to execute the processes on the relevant execution paths. Whilst the summation is straightforward, the calculation of the execution time for each process is less so. For example, the time taken to perform a channel communication consists of a time to execute an input or output operation together with the time required to synchronize the sender and receiver. This latter value depends on which operation is offered first and may cause an input or output process to wait. Thus the actual time required to perform an input–output operation depends on the timing of both of the processes involved. To satisfy real-time constraints the designer must ensure that processes on a critical path are not kept waiting, that is, the other partner in a communication must be waiting when the communication is offered. This can only be done by tailoring the hardware and software of the system to meet the timing required. The use of PRI ALT and PRI PAR ensures that the designer knows which process will be scheduled when the implementation has a choice.

One important design aim is to limit the real-time features of the system to a subset of all the processes. Since real-time processes are more difficult to design because of the timing constraints a good design will limit the real-time parts of the problem solution to as small a section as possible. Hence one technique used extensively is to encode as much time dependence as possible into the device drivers, which are responsible for dealing with any time constraints associated with servicing the hardware device, for example, the fact that a disc rotates and hence data can only be read or written at specific times when the head is in the correct position with respect to the disc surface.

Although it is not possible to determine all the parameters which affect timing in advance, for example, the number of times around a loop may depend on the input data, it is usually possible for the designer to calculate the worst case times and to ensure that these meet the timing constraints.

10.5 EXAMPLES

10.5.1 Regular Processing

One use of the delay process is to time the interval between sending control signal to other modules, that is, to generate a clock with a longer period than the system clock (Fig. 10.1).

```
DEF second = xx :  -- no of clock ticks per second
CHAN control :
VAR wakeuptime,command :
SEQ
  command := xx   -- set up command
  TIME ? wakeuptime -- get current time
  control ! command -- send command
  wakeuptime := wakeuptime + second
  WHILE TRUE
    SEQ
      TIME ? AFTER wakeuptime    -- wait for next time
      control ! command          -- send command
      wakeuptime := wakeuptime + second
```

Fig. 10.1 Processing in regular intervals in occam.

Notice that this program will output the command along the control channel at intervals of one second, subject to the accuracy of the clock. The constant second has to be set to the correct value for the particular implementation used.

10.5.2 Timing out of communications

In communicating systems it is often required to terminate the offer of communication after a set time to be able to deal with situations where the other process involved in the communication has terminated or crashed, or where there has been an error in the communication. In order to do this in occam we need some mechanism for an offer of communication to be abandoned after a period of time. This is provided by a mixture of the delay mechanism combined with the ALT construct. Consider the fragment of code shown in Fig. 10.2.

```
TIME ? t
ALT
  ch ? x
    -- action
  TIME ? AFTER (t + timeout)
    -- default action
```

Fig. 10.2 Timeout processing in occam.

The ALT construct provides a way for the process to wait for either an input on channel ch or for the specified delay. If both the timeout and the input on channel ch occurred 'at the same time' then the implementation could choose either associated action. If the user required one particular choice to be made under these circumstances then a PRI ALT could be used instead.

10.5.3 Message reception

We have seen that a process may receive a message over a channel by simply performing an input on the appropriate channel, for example,

```
ch ? x
```

This method of communication, however, causes the requesting process to wait until the sending process is ready to send. We have also seen that it is possible to time-out the communication after a set period of time (Fig. 10.3).

```
TIME ? x
ALT
  ch ? x
    -- perform action
  TIME ? AFTER (x + interval)
    -- perform time-out action
```

Fig. 10.3 Timing out communications in occam.

A related type of communication is where a process wishes to check to see if communication over a channel is waiting each time it enters a processing loop, that is it wishes to poll at the start of each execution of the loop. This can be done in occam by the code shown in Fig. 10.4.

```
WHILE TRUE
  SEQ
    ALT
      in ? message
        -- process message
      TRUE & SKIP
        SKIP
    -- perform normal processing
```

Fig. 10.4 Polling in occam.

Every time around the loop the ALT process is obeyed. The input guard will only be true if there is an input message waiting but the TRUE & SKIP guard will always be true thus ensuring that the process will not wait if no message is waiting. The problem with this solution is that if a message is waiting then there is no guarantee that it will be chosen in preference to other guard. To ensure that the input message has preference requires the use of PRI ALT instead of ALT.

10.5.4 Servicing high priority devices in parallel

If we consider the implementation of device drivers for high speed peripherals we see that the obvious structure to use is a PAR construct to run the device drivers, which may be extremely time critical, in parallel with the processing algorithms. We should obviously buffer the communication between the processing processes and the device drivers to smooth out any irregularities in data production or consumption but we must remember that, in the steady state, buffering will not increase the amount of data we can process. If we run these processes in parallel then we could program the structure as shown in Fig. 10.5.

```
PAR
  Devdriver1
  Devdriver2
  Devdriver3
    .
    .
  Algprocess1
  Algprocess2
    .
    .
```

Fig. 10.5 Servicing processes in parallel.

This, however, suffers from the problem that, unless we run each of these processes on a separate processor there is no guarantee that the device processes will get sufficient priority and hence I/O may not work correctly due to timing problems. To ensure that these processes do get the appropriate priority PAR should be replaced by PRI PAR. There are more problems if these processes are run on a transputer. For example, in this environment rescheduling of processes is only done when one of a small number of instructions is executed thus even when a higher priority process becomes runable because there is input to it, it may not be scheduled immediately. Such problems can cause considerable inconvenience to the real-time programmer since he has to know the low-level details of the implementation in order to calculate whether his code will satisfy the timing constraints.

10.5.5. An automated teller example

As a larger example we consider here the design of an automated cash dispensing machine. We show how the real-time features of the problem are encapsulated in a set of processes and how we limit the influence of real-time effects to a subset of the set of processes. As we shall see the order of operations in this example is mainly sequential, there is little concurrency. However, the example does illustrate many of the problems of designing such real-time systems.

The problem is to design an automated bank teller that will dispense cash if the customer enters the correct account number, correct identity number and correct amount. We shall assume a simplified machine with a digits keypad for input, a cash dispenser and signs which can be illuminated for entering the account number, amount and identity number and for repeating the last operation as the outputs.

Design

In order to limit the real-time effects of the program we start by assuming that the input and output devices are controlled by intelligent device drivers. These device drivers are responsible to dealing with the specific characteristics of the input–output device and thus limit some of the real-time constraints. Let us consider the design of the central controller which controls the order of operations of the input–output devices. The structure of this central controller program would look something like that shown in Fig. 10.6.

```
WHILE TRUE
  SEQ
    -- display 'enter account number'
    -- wait for number to be input
    -- validate no. by sending to central database site
    -- if number incorrect then display 'try again' and
       -- return to beginning of loop
    -- display 'enter identity no.'
    -- wait for number to be input
    -- validate no. by sending to central database
    -- if number incorrect then display 'try again' and
    -- go to input number again
    -- display 'enter amount'
    -- wait for number to be input
    -- validate no. by sending to central database
    -- if not correct then display 'try again' and go to
    -- input no. again
    -- send command to cash dispenser to dispense cash
```

Fig. 10.6 Program structure for automated teller.

This description can obviously be tidied up by using a PROC to display the appropriate message, waiting for input and validating it. We shall do this in our solution given later but our interest here is in the real-time aspects of the problem and how we solve them. We have assumed that the keyboard process deals with the keypad and converts the set of key depressions into an integer and also determines when the user has finished typing a number, for example, by monitoring the number of key depressions or by monitoring the use of a special key indicating the end of the number. As it stands the response of the system to a user's request will depend on the time it takes to authenticate the input values, the time for the control process to communicate with the device driver processes, the time for the device driver processes and the time of the actual devices themselves. As any user of a real cash dispenser system will know by far the largest of these times is the time required for the central database to respond to validation requests. This time is difficult to calculate since the database is shared amongst a large number of cash dispensers and is used for other purposes. Hence the response time depends on the global environment; the total number of processes trying to access the database. The response time of the rest of the system is simply a matter of calculating the sum of the execution times of the instructions involved. There is no waiting time involved here since the ordering of operations is essentially sequential, that is, the controller enables the keyboard and then immediately waits for a reply.

There is a problem, however, which the solution outlined above does not overcome. What happens if a user leaves the system in the middle of a transaction, for whatever reason? When another user attempts to use the system he will discover that he is in the middle of a transaction and may not be able to progress if the previous user has inserted his account number but not his identity number, or may be able to withdraw cash from the previous user's account if he abandoned the machine before requesting cash! There must therefore be some mechanism for resetting the system to its state at the beginning of the control loop. There are a number of ways of performing this, all of which involve the use of the time-out facility. Firstly, the keyboard process could be programmed so that it times-out after a given period of time with no input in the middle of a transaction and reports this to the control process which could then revert to its idle state. Again this is reasonable because the time before the system reverted to its idle state could be easily computed from the code. A second technique would be for the keyboard to include a special clear key which, when depressed, caused the system to revert to its idle state. This solution could cause more problems for the implementor since in essence this is an 'interrupt' key, that is whatever the system is doing it should abandon it and revert to its idle state. As we have described previously interrupts are not provided in occam; the user has to explicitly poll for events. Thus the solution outlined above would have to be modified so that output from the keyboard process was looked at at particular points in the code to detect if the clear key had been depressed. As we have already stated in a real system the time consuming step would be the access to the central database. If we wished the user to be able to abort his transaction during access to the central database then this communication would have to be timed out and the communication channel to the keyboard examined to see if the user had hit the clear key. If the user had not hit the clear key then the original database communication could be resumed, otherwise the system would have to be reset after the database transaction had ended. We consider the simple timeout solution first (Fig. 10.7).

```
DEF eacno = 1, pin = 2, amount = 3, -- display codes
    timeout = ???,  -- keyboard time out data response
    touttime = ???, -- time out interval
    on = ???, off = ???,  -- defs for display on or off
    secs = ??? :


CHAN activatecd, dispeacno, disppin,
     dispamount, dispagain,  -- i/o channels
     kch,           -- data channel to keyboard
     db,dbreply :  -- channels to database process

PROC controller =
  WHILE TRUE             -- loop forever
    VAR tmout,rply :
    SEQ
      display(eacno,tmout,rply) -- display enter acc no
      IF
        NOT(tmout)              -- if not timed out
          SEQ
            display(pin,tmout,rply) -- display enter PIN
            IF
              NOT(tmout)
                SEQ
                  display(amount,tmout,rply)      -- enter
                                               -- display amount
                  IF
                    NOT(tmout)
                      activatcd ! rply  -- start cash disp'er
                    TRUE
                      SKIP
              TRUE
                SKIP
        TRUE
          SKIP  :

PROC display(VALUE type, VAR tmout,rply) =
  VAR doagain :
  SEQ
    doagain := TRUE
    WHILE doagain
      VAR val :
      SEQ
        IF
          type = eacno    -- send message to light display
            dispeacno ! on
          type = pin
```

Continued

Continued

```
            disppin ! on
          type = amount
            dispamount ! on
          TRUE
            SKIP
        keyboard(val)  -- read value from keyboard
        dispagain ! off -- set display of
        IF
          type = eacno  -- set other display off
            dispeacno ! off
          type = pin
            disppin ! off
          type = amount
            dispamount ! off
          TRUE
            SKIP
        IF
          val = timeout   -- if keyboard timed out
            SEQ
              doagain := FALSE  -- exit loop
              tmout := TRUE     -- with tmout true
          TRUE
            VAR torf :
            SEQ
              tmout := FALSE  -- else tmout is false
              db ! type ; val -- send to database
              dbreply ? torf  -- reply true of false
              IF
                NOT(torf)     -- reply false
                  dispagain ! on  -- ask user to reinput
                TRUE
                  SEQ
                    doagain := FALSE  -- reply true so
                    rply := val  :    -- exit loop

PROC keyboard(VAR digval) =
  VAR ndig  :
  SEQ
    ndig := 0    -- no of digits input
    digval := 0  -- and integer value
    WHILE ndig < 4  -- user has to input 4 digits
      VAR curtime,d :
      SEQ
        TIME ? curtime
        ALT
          kch ? d  -- read value at update total
            SEQ
              ndig := ndig + 1
              digval := (digval * 10) + d - '0'
          TIME ? AFTER curtime + (touttime * secs) -- time out
            SEQ
              ndig := 5            -- get out of loop
              digval := timeout  :-- with time out value

SEQ
  controller
```

Fig. 10.7 occam code for automated teller using time outs.

Notice that this solution for the controller is completely sequential; there is no concurrency as the problem has been specified although some could have been introduced if, for example, the database interrogation takes too long it could be handled by a parallel buffer construct but normally, in this situation, the database processor would be tuned so that it responds in a reasonable time.

Turning now to the alternative solution proposed, the introduction of a clear key which would allow the user to return to the initial dialog from any state of the machine. In fact a moments thought should convince you that this is not a sensible solution since the only way in which the flow of control can be modified to cope with the user not performing the intended series of actions is to time out communications and check the status of the clear key. However, timing out the communication as above is sufficient for restoring the system to its initial state; the pressing of the clear button is superfluous.

An Aside

However, consideration of a clear button does lead to an interesting situation which is worthy of consideration. Consider the case where a validation request has been sent to the database but the response has not been received. The user may decide that he cannot wait any longer and presses the reset button. In order to detect this action the controller has to accept either a response from the database or the reset channel. If a response from the reset channel is received first then the controller can take one of two actions; it can remember this fact and discard the database reply when received or it can attempt to cancel the command given to the database. Considering the latter case first, we have the situation in Fig. 10.8.

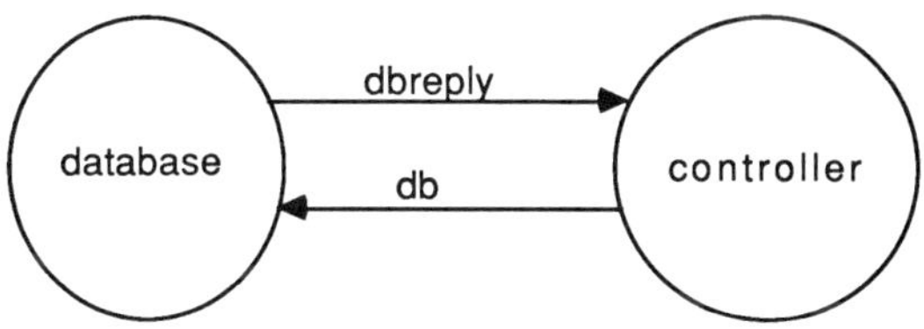

Fig. 10.8 Solution to exhibiting a timing problem.

The problem is that any cancel command to the database may overlap in time with the database reply since the processes are asynchronous. This is likely to lead to deadlock if both processes commit themselves to sending at the same time. A solution is to interpose a more complicated protocol between the processes, such as a semaphore, but this produces a complex solution. If we now consider the other possible solution, remembering to ignore the next reply from the database, this is also reasonably difficult to implement. Since the reply from the database is asynchronous the communication channel has to be buffered so that the reply can always be accepted, the database process must be prepared to wait until the controller process is ready to accept the reply or the database process can time out and remember to resend the last piece of data at a later time. Each of these alternatives has its own problems but the buffered communications channel is the easiest to program. The same problem then arises when the system is reinitialized as the buffer has to be initialized and the database has to be informed to cancel its current transaction. Solving these problems are not insuperable, for example, the database process could flush the communications buffer when it was initialized but the complications can give rise to more complicated programmed solutions. Especially in real-time systems, it is important to keep the system as simple as possible consistent with the requirements. It is worth noting here that the complications outlined above occur because the database process is not responding quickly enough. A simple solution is to implement the database process on a fast computer which satisfies the constraints without the need to resort to timing out for speed purposes.

It is worth considering this last example in a little more detail as regards to real-time constraints. Since the controller process is sequential and, we assume, always ready to accept input from the user in response to a request then the only difficulty in predicting the response time, assuming that the performance of the hardware is known and catered for, is to estimate the response time of the database to validation requests. In an example such as this the response time of the system would be measured, assuming that the database process already existed, or limits on its performance would be placed on the designers if it did not. The performance of this system can then be estimated by summing the code required to perform the tasks.

10.5.6. A simple controller/sensor example

As the last example in this section we will consider a simple control application which has some real-time constraints. We will only consider a small part of the complete system here but the extensions to a complete system are relatively simple. We assume that with each controller/monitoring unit is associated a monitoring process which both controls the action of the unit and monitors the data produced. The monitoring process is connected to an operator process which issues commands to stop and start the unit and receives monitored sensor data together with an indication of whether the data is valid, as described below, together

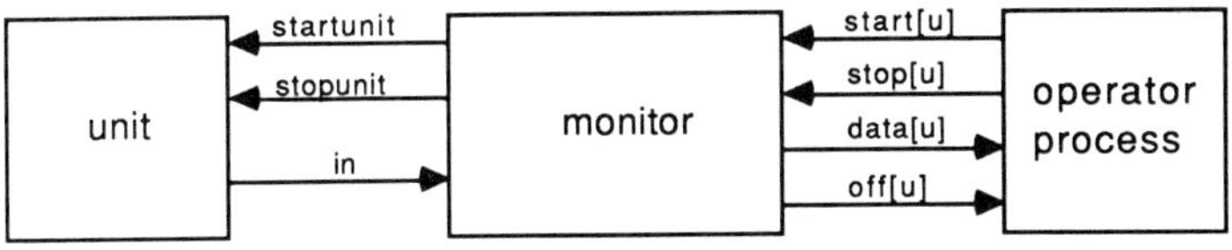

Fig. 10.9 Block diagram of a real-time system.

with signals indicating that the sub-system has stopped (Fig. 10.9).

The channels between the operator process and the monitor are indexed so that the operator process can control multiple monitors. The operation of the monitor can be described as follows: when the monitor receives a start[u] signal it sends a startunit signal to the unit and then relays data from channel in to channel data[u] together with an indication of whether the data exceeds a given bound b. If data values do not fall below bound b within time t the unit is stopped. The unit may also be stopped at any time by a stop[u] signal from the operator process. The operator process is informed via off[u] when the unit has been stopped for any reason.

One of the main concerns in the design of the monitor code is to check the input signals from the operator process sufficiently often, for example, stop[u] to stop the unit (Fig. 10.10).

When the monitor is activated it first ensures that the controller/sensor unit is in a stopped state. It does this by sending a stopunit signal to the unit and waiting for an acknowledgement to this appearing on the in data channel. Having done this it informs the operator process that the unit has stopped by a signal on the off[u] channel. The monitor is then ready to perform its function and sits in an infinite loop accepting inputs from the operator process and the unit. Initially the only input requiring attention is a start[u] signal from the operator process. On receipt of such a signal the monitor sends a startunit signal to the unit and sits in a loop basically collecting and forwarding data from the unit to the operator process. Exit from this loop has to occur when the unit is stopped either because of an operator process command or because the output from the sensor unit has been above bound *b* for longer than time *t*. The Boolean variable intiming is used to signify whether the previous data value was above the bound *b* or not. When the data value increases above bound *b* a reference time is read from the special channel TIME and this value, with the time out period *t* added, is then used in a guard to detect when time out has occurred. The use of the PRI ALT construct is to ensure that the two conditions for stopping the unit, timeout and operator process command, have priority over data input from the unit. There is potentially a major problem here, similar to the previous example. When the monitor process wishes to stop the unit it issues a stopunit signal. However, there is no guarantee that the unit is willing to accept this input

```
PROC monitor(VALUE u,b,t,CHAN stopunit,startunit,in,
             start[],stop[],data[],off[]) =

  PROC stopio =
    VAR stopack :
    SEQ
      stopunit ! ANY          -- send stop to unit
      stopack := FALSE
      WHILE NOT(stopack)      -- wait for acknowledge
        in ? stopack  :

  DEF t = ?? :                -- time out time
  SEQ
    stopio                    -- stop unit
    off[u] ! ANY
    WHILE TRUE
      ALT
        stop[u] ? ANY
          off[u] ! ANY
        in ? ANY
          SKIP              -- should not happen, error
        start[u] ? ANY
          VAR intiming,stopped :
          SEQ
            startunit ! ANY       -- start the unit
            intiming := FALSE
            stopped := FALSE      -- boolean for timed out
            WHILE NOT(stopped)
              VAR reftime :
              PRI ALT
                intiming & TIME ? AFTER (reftime + t)--time out
                  SEQ
                    stopio                  -- stop unit
                    off[u] ! ANY            -- inform operator
                    stopped := TRUE         -- out of loop
                stop[u] ? ANY
                  SEQ
                    stopio
                    off[u] ! ANY    -- inform operator
                    stopped := TRUE -- set boolean
                start[u] ? ANY
                  SKIP              -- already started
                in ? val
                  VAR ok :
                  SEQ
                    ok := (val<b)
                    data[u] ! val;ok -- send data and validity
                    IF
                      NOT(ok) AND NOT(intiming) -- first time
                        SEQ                     -- out of range
                          TIME ? reftime   -- set time out time
                          intiming := TRUE -- timing
                      ok
                        intiming := FALSE  -- not timing
                      TRUE
                        SKIP :
```

Fig. 10.10 occam code for real-time controller.

at the time it is issued. Furthermore, the unit may be committed to outputting data at the same time as the monitor is committed to sending the stop signal. This will result in deadlock. There are a number of solutions to this but in this case the best one is probably to constrain the designer of the controller/sensor unit to give priority to control inputs and to scan the inputs between every data output. If this is adhered to then the only requirement for correct action is for the unit output to be single buffered.

In effect the data unit should behave like the following process in Fig. 10.11 with the data channel single buffered.

```
PROC unit(CHAN stopin,startin,data) =
  WHILE TRUE
    VAR endofdata :
    PRI ALT
      stopin ? ANY
        -- take stop action
        data ! stopack
      startin ? ANY
        -- take start action
        endofdata := TRUE
        WHILE NOT(endofdata)
          PRI ALT
            stopin ? ANY
              -- take stop action
              endofdata := TRUE
              data ! stopack
            TRUE
              -- generate next data value
              data ! val :    -- send data to buffer
```

Fig. 10.11 Model of unit behaviour in occam.

SUMMARY Chapter 10

In this chapter the use of occam in real-time systems has been considered. Occam provides some features in the language to facilitate real-time programming, for example, the TIME channel and the PRI ALT construct. Whilst these extra constructs are useful for producing real-time programs, the design of such systems is notoriously difficult and although the concurrency features of occam help in expressing concurrency in the solution producing solutions to real-time problems is still difficult.

EXERCISES Chapter 10

E10.1 Reconsider the simple operating system discussed in Chapter 10. Which parts of the code would you inspect carefully to ensure that the system responded as quickly as possible? Can you see any changes which could be made to the code to improve the real-time characteristics of the system?

E10.2 Considering the operating system problem again, how would you code the device process if the readers were changed for visual display units with operators having the ability to type ahead?

E10.3 With reference to the final example above, the simple controller/sensor, rewrite the code so that instead of using two channels, stopunit and startunit, to the unit only one channel called control is used with signals (ANY) on the channel meaning a change of control action from started to stopped or vice versa.

11

HIGHER LEVEL COMMUNICATION PRIMITIVES

So far we have modelled the basic interaction between processes in terms of the occam communication primitives ! and ? over a channel. As has been shown in this text these are low-level primitives leaving the programmer with a substantial programming task to produce the required communication protocol for a distributed solution to a real problem. In occam this manifests itself in many examples by the necessity of using a large number of different channels. In order to simplify the programming task a more sophisticated communications primitive is required. However, it must be borne in mind that one of the aims of programming is to produce systems which are easy to use, understand and reason about. Hence the need for any new communication primitives to have a sound mathematical basis.

11.1 DECOUPLING

In the buffer examples considered previously the information flow between producer and consumer was queued thus decoupling them so that they could run asynchronously. A simple extension to occam to incorporate this type of decoupling would be to incorporate buffers in the channels to decouple the input and output process by a given amount, for example,

```
CHAN[d] a,b,c  :
```

where d is a static constant >=0 indicating the amount of decoupling on the channels. Hence

d = 0, fully synchronous; a standard occam channel
d = 1, singly decoupled (c.f. buffer with d=1)
d > 1, multiply decoupled (c.f. buffer with d>1)

If we have these types of channels then they may potentially be shared between **multiple** processes, since the buffer implements the correct synchronization. This suggestion is attributed to S. Jaehnichen of G.M.D. Karlsruhe.

This extension to the occam communication primitives aids the programmer in that buffers are not now explicitly required, but more help in the reduction of the number of channels is required. For this we need to consider a further extension to occam.

11.2 CHANNEL SHARING

In the occam model communication channels are statically defined, unidirectional and dedicated to a pair of processes, that is, only a single process may read from and a single process write to a channel. Therefore, processes cannot share channels. This results in most occam programs requiring a large number of channels and the code to manage them. The channel requirements can be reduced if channel sharing is allowed. It should be noted that this implies a change in the basic mathematical model on which the language is based. The communication semantics of the new model are now nearer CCS (Milner, 1980), than those of CSP (Hoare, 1985).

If channels are to be shared then there is a possibility that multiple input or output processes may access a single channel simultaneously and therefore communications may clash. We define the action of the channel in this case to be **serialization**, that is, that the channel mechanism will ensure that a maximum of only one input and one output process can access a channel simultaneously; multiple requests will be sequenced in an undefined order.

In the following we assume that channels are still unidirectional but that they may be shared by any number of processes. Using this scheme the semaphore solutions given as Examples 7 and 8 now become legal, as do the buffer examples for multiple producers and consumers, as shown in Fig. 11.1.

In fact, channel sharing means that multiplexers and demultiplexers are redundant in any example since they are now included in the channels.

Consideration of the buffer example using an array of single slot buffers leads to a slightly different solution using shared channels. The occam solution given in Chapter 4 may be modified using shared channels (Fig. 11.2).

```
DEF n = ... :   -- number of writers
DEF m = ... :   -- number of readers
CHAN w,r :
PAR

  -- single slot buffer

  WHILE TRUE
    VAR b :
    SEQ
      w?b
      r!b

  -- interface protocols

  PROC put(VALUE v) =
    w!v :

  PROC get(VAR v) =
    r?v :

  -- client protocols

  PAR
    PAR i = [0 FOR n]
      VAR x :
      .... put(x) ....

    PAR i = [0 FOR m]
      VAR y :
      .... get(y) ....
```

Fig. 11.1 Single slot buffer for multiple readers and writers using shared channels.

There is a difference between this solution and that given previously; senders and receivers take offers of communication in any order, that is, the ordering of data on the channels is dependent on the underlying serialization mechanism. In the previous solution the requests for slots were ordered in time but the usage of the buffer was not necessarily so ordered. In most cases this distinction is not important since most applications do not rely on a strict FIFO buffer regime.

It is instructive to consider the crossbar switch example of Chapter 5 using shared channels. In the occam solution there were n × m channels directly connecting all the input processes to all the output processes and two channels from each process to the central scheduler for requesting a connection and receiving an index. Using shared channels a simple solution is to remove the central scheduler and multiplex the n × m channels to a single shared channel. This solution is elegant and simple but only works for single transactions since two successive writes from one output process may be received by different input processes.

To solve the problem for multiple transactions an **intelligent** multiplexer/demultiplexer is required on the shared channel or an external control system is necessary to enforce the required mutual exclusion of channel use. Since the former solution is equivalent to sending data

```
DEF n = ... :    -- number of writers
DEF m = ... :    -- number of readers
DEF d = ... :    -- number of buffers
CHAN r,w :
PAR

  -- communication buffer

  PAR i = [0 FOR d]
    WHILE TRUE
      VAR b :
      SEQ
        w?b
        r!b

  -- interface protocols

  PROC put( VALUE v ) =
    w!v :

  PROC get( VAR v ) =
    r?v :

  -- client processes

  PAR
    PAR i = [0 FOR n]
      VAR x :
      .... put(x) ....

    PAR i = [0 FOR m]
      VAR y :
      .... get(y) ....    :
```

Fig. 11.2 Multi-slot buffer for multiple readers and writers using shared channels.

through the scheduler, a solution we rejected in the original case, we will not consider this further here. Considering the latter case, we require a solution which is very similar to the original crossbar switch example, except that we only require a single shared channel instead of the n × m dedicated channels.

A number of other modifications can be seen in this example. Since we have only a single dedicated channel between all the producers and consumers the scheduler does not have to calculate which channel to use, only to signal that the shared channel may be used. Another change required is for both the producer and consumer to signal to the scheduler when they have finished with the shared channel so that the scheduler knows when it can be reallocated. This was not required in the former case because channels were dedicated to specific pairs of processes. This signalling can be done on the request lines since request for allocation and deallocation come in order and thus the scheduler knows the type of request from the ordering. Thus the number of channels required here is considerably reduced, but at the cost of some concurrency since only one transaction can take place at any given time. Allowing more concurrency

```
DEF n = ... :  -- number of writers
DEF m = ... :  -- number of readers
CHAN pconnectionreq[n],cconnectionreq[m],
     crossconnection :
PAR
  WHILE TRUE
    SEQ
      ALT i=[0 FOR n]
        pconnectionreq[i]?ANY -- wait for req
          SKIP
      ALT j=[0 FOR m]
        cconnectionreq[j]?ANY -- wait for req
          SKIP
      pconnectionreq?ANY -- wait for end of use
      cconnectionreq?ANY

  -- producers

  PAR i=[0 FOR n]
    WHILE TRUE
      SEQ
        pconnectionreq[i]!ANY
            .
            .
        pconnectionreq[i]!ANY

  -- consumers

  PAR i=[0 FOR m]
    WHILE TRUE
      SEQ
        cconnectionreq[i]!ANY
            .
            .
        cconnectionreq[i]!ANY
```

Fig. 11.3 Code for intelligent multiplexer/demultiplexer using shared channels.

means adding more shared channels and allocating their use by a scheduler as before.

If we now consider the case where the producer wishes to send to a specific consumer a simple solution exists. We could use the occam code above and modify the scheduler so that after accepting a producer request it will only accept a request from the named consumer (Fig. 11.4).

We are assured that this solution will work since the shared channel can

```
DEF n = ... :  -- number of producers
VAR consumerid :
WHILE TRUE
  SEQ
    ALT i=[0 FOR n]
      pconnectionreq[i]?consumerid
        SKIP
    cconnectionreq[consumerid]?ANY
    pconnectionreq[i]?ANY
    cconnectionreq[i]?ANY
```

Fig. 11.4 Modification for named consumer.

only be used by a single producer and consumer at a time and therefore all the other processes must be idle, that is, the consumer process must be free waiting for a scheduler response when the scheduler requires it. This raises the problem outlined above; a single shared channel does not allow concurrent use by multiple producers and consumers. How do we overcome this? In the case of specific consumers one solution is to provide an input channel which is connected to all the producers. Hence any producer outputting on that channel is guaranteed to go to a particular consumer. A control system is now required to ensure that a particular producer has exclusive use of the channel for multiple transactions. Assuming that a scheduler is provided for each shared channel then the code for a solution is shown in Fig. 11.5.

We could not use a single shared channel for all the communication to the scheduler since all inputs over the shared channel are serialized thus giving no guarantee that the signal from a producer deallocating the channel will immediately follow the allocation to the same process; other input processes from other producers might be interleaved. Hence the only way in which the scheduler can guarantee to receive the request to deallocate the channel before the next request is by the use of a separate channel.

```
DEF n = ... :   -- number of producers
DEF m = ... :   -- number of consumers
CHAN schedulerreq, schedulerfree,consumerin[m]:
PAR

  -- scheduler processes

  PAR i=[0 FOR m]
    WHILE TRUE
      SEQ
        schedulerreq?ANY
        schedulerfree?ANY

  --  producers

  PAR i = [0 FOR n]
    WHILE TRUE
      SEQ
        schedulerreq!ANY
        -- use shared channel
           .
           .
           .
        schedulerfree!ANY

  --  consumers

  PAR i = [0 FOR m]
    WHILE TRUE
      SEQ
        consumerin[i]?x
           .
        -- process x
           .
```

Fig. 11.5 Concurrent use of shared channels.

Returning to the problem of concurrent communication between sets of anonymous processes performing multiple transactions over shared channels, we are confronted by the fact that we need multiple channels for concurrent communication. We could use shared channels rather than dedicated ones but this does not give us any advantage in this case since we still need a scheduler to organize their use. We would, however, reduce the number of channels required since the maximum concurrency means that we would not require n × m channels, only max(m,n).

Thus we have shown that shared channels can provide some extra power to the user in some cases, giving him a richer primitive with which to construct programs. This primitive is simple to implement although the implementor must be careful to ensure that it is fair. We have also seen that the use of even this primitive is still rather tricky and requires the programmer to deal with a number of difficult synchronization problems. As we shall see in our next model, which uses procedural call–return mechanisms rather than input–output primitives, a higher level primitive makes programming easier.

11.3 RENDEZVOUS

A standard mechanism for abstraction in sequential programming languages is the subroutine or procedure. At some place in the code a call to a procedure is executed and control is passed to that procedure, together with any required parameters. On exit from the procedure any output parameters are copied back to the calling procedure and that procedure continues from the point of the call. The effect is just as though the called procedure code had been executed in line at the calling point.

The rendezvous, the basis of communication in the Ada language (ADA, 1982), is a similar communication mechanism in a concurrent programming environment. In this case calls are between two concurrent processes and the rendezvous takes place when one process calls an entry in another process *and* when the called process reaches an accept for the same entry. The two processes are then synchronized and the called process then performs any actions required just as if it were called as a procedure. Only when the called process has finished with the call is the calling process allowed to proceed. Thus the rendezvous mechanism mirrors the procedure call in sequential languages and, like that mechanism, can be nested, that is, processes may call processes which call other processes and so on, hierarchically. In terms of the other communication mechanisms considered so far the rendezvous acts as a shared channel, that is, calls to entry points may occur from many places in different processes but they are accepted sequentially. Since the call may include parameters it is at a higher level than the occam channel. Furthermore there is an implied synchronization which forces the caller to wait until the called process has **finished** the rendezvous, not just until the call has been accepted.

To illustrate the concept of the rendezvous, similar to that in the Ada language, we give some examples in an extended higher level notation. In this notation we use named loops with specific **iter** statements which cause iteration back to the start of the named loop. We rename the ALT construct as **opt** with guarded statements replaced by @ and an entry, including parameters if necessary. The rest of the notation is similar to a typical high-level language and should be readable without further explanation.

As a simple example consider the single slot buffer (Exercise 4). Recoded in this new notation using rendezvous it becomes as shown in Fig. 11.6.

```
par
  var x :
  while true do
    @put(x)            ; sequentially accept puts
    @get(->y)          ; followed by gets
      y := x
  par
    par i = [0 for n]
      var x :
      ...... call put(x) ......
    par i = [0 for m]
      var y :
      ...... call get(y) ......
```

Fig. 11.6 Single slot buffer coded in the new notation.

The higher level notation does not help to simplify this small example; the solution is simply a translation into a different notation.

As a further example consider the courier example. If we restrict ourselves to a single courier initially the producers and consumers reduce to a single call an entry in the courier to send or receive a message. One possible coding of the courier is shown in Fig. 11.7 where the courier continually loops through the rendezvous, firstly with the producer and secondly with the consumer. The courier buffers the value between producer and consumer as the single slot buffer above. Another possible encoding is shown in Fig. 11.8.

Here the producer is held in rendezvous for the complete transaction

```
while true do
  @ prod(z)
  @ cons(->y)
      y := z
```

Fig. 11.7 A courier coded in the new notation.

```
while true do
  @prod(z)
    @cons(->y)
      y := z
```

Fig. 11.8 A different coding of the courier.

and the courier does not actually store anything; it simply acts as a synchronizer between producer and consumer and the data passes directly between them.

If we now consider the case where there are multiple couriers then we have a problem in determining which courier to use. The solution is to use a separate scheduler as before.

11.4 RENDEZVOUS WITH CONTINUATIONS

The rendezvous described in the previous section suffers from a particular problem; the called process must complete the rendezvous with the caller before it can accept another rendezvous from another caller. But this behaviour cannot solve problems such as the Bankers Algorithm (Dijkstra, 1965). In this type of resource algorithm a manager manages a fixed set of resources and responds to requests to obtain and release a given number of resources – to deposit and withdraw cash at a bank in the original example. If there is not enough of the resource available, instead of informing the consumer of failure and letting him request again later, the algorithm makes him wait (queues him). In programming terms this means the manager process holding the consumer process in rendezvous but still being able to receive requests to release resources from other processes. We extend the rendezvous notation to deal with this situation by the addition of **continuations**. In the examples which follow we use **pass as** to denote continuations, that is, where the rendezvous ends as far as the called process is concerned but where the caller is still held in rendezvous.

Using the notation for rendezvous described in the last section the solution to the Bankers Algorithm can be described as shown in Fig. 11.9.

Here the continuation is entered if there are not enough resources available to satisfy the caller. The call in the continuation will eventually be released from its rendezvous which will release the original caller from the initial rendezvous. To illustrate the working of this solution consider a specific example. There are ten blocks of memory available and a caller requests six. Six are allocated to the caller since n = < avail is true and the number of blocks still available is reduced to four. The next request is for five blocks and this cannot be satisfied since there are only four available. In this case the number of waiting callers is incremented,

```
loop manager do
  opt
      @request(n)
        if n =< avail
        then avail := avail - n
                -- grant request and update state
        else waiting := waiting + 1
                pass as call defer(n)
  or   @release(n)
        avail := avail + n
        if waiting # 0
        then @defer(n)
             if n =< avail
             then avail := avail - n
                  waiting := waiting - 1
                  -- grant req and update state
             else pass as call defer(n)
```

Fig. 11.9 The Bankers Algorithm coded in the new notation.

setting it to one, and the caller is still held in the rendezvous until the call to defer can be satisfied although the manager is released to accept other calls. Another call to request less than four blocks would be satisfied and the caller released but calls requesting more than this number would be held in rendezvous, all waiting for the call defer to succeed. When a caller releases some blocks the manager process updates the free block count and then checks to see if any callers are being held in continuations by checking the waiting count. In this example the caller releases five blocks and there is a process in the continuation so the manager accepts the call to defer, checks if there are enough blocks available now, which there are, and allocates them, thus releasing the process from the continuation and the original caller from the rendezvous. If the deferred request could not have been satisfied then the manager would have deferred it again.

As a second example consider the case of a snapshot arbiter where requests for a resource are accumulated over a period of time and then dealt with in some sequence. This is what happens in some hardware arbiters where there are concurrent requests for the use of a scarce resource, for example, a bus.

The simplest solution is shown in Fig. 11.10 but this solution does not

```
loop arbiter do
  opt
      @request(n)
        id[n] := true
  or   @clk
         loop disp set i from 1 to n do
           if id[i] = true
           then dispatch(i)
                id[i] := false
           iter disp
  iter arbiter
```

Fig. 11.10 A snapshot arbiter coded in the new notation.

hold the caller whilst the dispatching takes place. To do this we need to use continuations (Fig. 11.11).

```
loop arbiter do
  opt
      @request(n)
        waiting := waiting + 1
        pass as call free(n)
  or  @clk
        while waiting # 0 do
          @free(n)
          dispatch(n)
          waiting := waiting - 1
  iter arbiter
```

Fig. 11.11 A modified snapshot arbiter.

Note that this solution assumes a first-come-first-served scheduling discipline. To implement any other scheme is more difficult; try it as an exercise.

SUMMARY Chapter 11

We have seen in this chapter that the simple communication model of occam, whilst providing the basic mechanism of synchronized communication, is a low-level construct. Higher level constructs make the programmers task easier and less error prone. However, it is still not clear exactly what is the best form of communication primitive. Here we have suggested rendezvous with continuations as being one possible model for a higher level communications primitive.

EXERCISES Chapter 11

E11.1 A synchronization problem, first suggested by Brinch Hansen, is the vending machine example. A vending machine accepts one of two actions which may not occur concurrently: depositing a coin in a slot or pressing a button to obtain an item. If the button is pressed the vending machine will dispense an item provided that sufficient money has previously been inserted and the machine is not empty; otherwise any money deposited is returned. Write an occam program to simulate this situation. Can the solution be simplified using any of the modifications suggested in this chapter and if so how?

E11.2 Dijkstra first suggested a problem, called the Dining Philosophers' problem, which requires facilities for mutual exclusion for its solution. In this problem five philosophers are seated around a circular table with a fork placed between each philosopher. In order to eat a philosopher must acquire the two forks immediately to his left and right. Assuming that a philosopher will not release a fork once it has been picked up until he has finished eating, if each philosopher acquires a single fork then deadlock occurs since nobody can acquire two forks. The problem is to write a program, in this case in occam, to allow the philosophers to eat without deadlock occurring. Would the use of the extensions to occam suggested in this chapter aid the solution? For those who wish for a harder challenge, produce a solution which is fair, that is, which ensures that no philosopher waits indefinitely.

12

FURTHER READING

Occam is a relatively new language and there is therefore relatively little published material on the language. The book written by Inmos Ltd. (Inmos Ltd., 1985) is the standard reference manual for the language. This refers to the first version of the language used in this book. A tutorial guide to occam 2 by Pountain and May (Pountain and May, 1987) and a text on occam with examples (Kerridge, 1987) have just been published as this book is being written. Various other books on occam are rumoured to be in various stages of publication although none has appeared at the time of writing. Articles on various topics related to occam are starting to appear in the computing literature but they are widely distributed so there is no simple way of searching the literature for them. An occam user group exists and holds regular meetings discussing uses and developments of the occam language and the transputer.

Whilst the occam language is comparatively recent, the first commercial implementations only becoming available in the last five years, the topic of concurrency is very much older. Concurrency first came into prominence in computing in the 1960's when multi-tasking operating systems first became available. The idea of multiple processes running on a single processor brought to light many of the problems of concurrent systems and initiated much of the original work on concurrency, although the concurrency could only be simulated on a single processor. It was not, however, until the advent of cheap microprocessors and the emergence of computer systems built from collections of these components about ten years ago that there was a reawakening of interest in concurrency and a new interest in pursuing research into real concurrency.

The type of concurrency to be found in operating systems is well represented in the literature in the wide range of texts available. Two of the more recent textbooks on operating systems which include a good coverage of concurrency topics are Peterson and Silberschatz (1985) and (Deitel,

1983). Textbooks covering a broader range of concurrency issues are much scarcer and Hwang and Briggs (1986) is probably the most comprehensive.

Most of the major computing journals, for example, the *Journal of the ACM* and *ACM Transactions on Computer Systems* often report theoretical and practical work on concurrency and journals such as *Distributed Computing* and the *Journal of Parallel Processing* are almost exclusively concerned with topics related to concurrency.

Many conferences are now dedicated to concurrency and associated topics. Perhaps the most important ones which occur regularly are the International Conferences on Distributed Computing Systems, sponsored by the I.E.E.E., and the Distributed Processing conferences and workshops organized by WG10.3 of I.F.I.P.

A substantial part of the Alvey and ESPRIT research and development programmes are concerned with concurrency in its various aspects. *Alvey News* contains reports of Alvey projects and the annual Alvey conference reports on the progress of the projects. Similarly ESPRIT projects are reported in the annual ESPRIT Technical Week and the proceedings are published.

CHAPTER 1

This chapter is concerned with some of the basic concepts of concurrency. A good general survey article on the topic of concepts and notations in concurrent programming is Andrews and Schneider (1983). The best sources of general information on these topics in the context of operating systems are Peterson and Silberschatz (1985), Brinch Hansen (1973) and Tanenbaum (1987), while Attwood (1976) discusses the types of concurrency found in operating systems. The survey article by Horning and Randell (1973), whilst relatively old, is still the best overall paper on the process concept. Process communication is also dealt with in the operating system books mentioned above and also by Sloman and Kramer (1987), who give a good account of bidirectional communication methods. Much of the original work on synchronization was performed by Dijkstra (Dijkstra, 1965; Dijkstra, 1968; Dijkstra, 1971) but Hoare (Hoare, 1974; Hoare, 1978) and Brinch Hansen (Brinch Hansen, 1972; Brinch Hansen, 1973) have also contributed significantly to developments in this area. In the deadlock area it was again Dijkstra (Dijkstra, 1965) who was one of the most influential workers although Holt (Holt, 1972) was the first person to formalize the notion of deadlock. Isloor and Marsland (1980) have written a survey article on the deadlock problem. Recent work in this area is almost exclusively concerned with distributed computing and interested readers are referred to the literature quoted at the beginning of this chapter.

CHAPTER 2

This chapter describes the programming language occam. Inmos Ltd (1985) is the standard text on the original version of the language as used in this book. Jones (1985) describes the language and the construction of a number of different programs including Conway's Game of Life and a Huffman coding example. May (1986) describes how occam is compiled for the transputer and May and Shepherd (1985) describe the way in which occam relates to a transputer. So far no text has been published on the transputer itself although literature is available from Inmos. A tutorial introduction to the latest version of the occam language, called occam 2 (Pountain and May, 1987) has just been published.

The occam language is based on the work of Hoare. A forerunner of the language is presented in Hoare (1978). Hoare's group at Oxford have more recently been working on the theory underlying the language and a book on this theory, called *Communicating Sequential Processes*, has been published (Hoare, 1985).

CHAPTERS 3 AND 4

In these chapters a number of different communication schemes are modelled in occam. Some of the references quoted for Chapter 1 are relevant, especially Sloman and Kramer (1987). The book by Ben-Ari (1982) is devoted to the problems of interprocess communication and includes many examples. The readers'/writers' problem for shared variables was first suggested by Courtois *et al.* (1971) and has since been explored by a large number of workers. The buffer example was first suggested by Dijkstra (1965) and, again, has been the subject of study by many workers in the field. Dijkstra, (Dijkstra, 1965; Dijkstra, 1968; Dijkstra, 1971) and Habermann (Habermann, 1972) discussed the various aspects of binary and general semaphores.

CHAPTER 5

Modelling of a crossbar switch and a courier connection is the subject of this chapter. Hwang and Briggs (1984) give details of the crossbar switch as used in computer architectures as do most texts dealing with multiprocessor architectures. The name 'courier' is reported to have been coined by R. C. Holt of Toronto University.

CHAPTER 6

This chapter is concerned with the techniques used in networking. As such the best reference is a good text on networking such as Tanenbaum (1981). Much of the nomenclature comes from the telecommunications industry since this was the first widespread use of large area networks.

CHAPTER 7

This chapter is concerned with the modelling of digital logic. There are two different types of simulator in use for modelling digital logic; an event based model (Milne, 1985; Hayes, 1986) and an assertional or axiomatic model (Gordon, 1981; Hanna and Daeche, 1985; and Moszkowski, 1983). In the first type of model the circuit is modelled by simulating the flow of data through the network of circuit elements as would happen in a real circuit whilst in the second type of model formal mathematical techniques are used to deduce properties of the system. Digital circuit simulators based on the first approach are very common and have been used in industry for many years, for example (Duley and Dietmeyer, 1968; Flake *et al.*, 1981 and Hayes, 1986). These are sequential, single processor implementations of a simulator. Some work has been performed on implementing such simulators on distributed systems, for example Misra (1986) and Peacock (1979), in order to see if the execution time of such simulators can be reduced.

CHAPTER 8

How to implement data structures as sets of processes rather than as passive objects is the subject of this chapter. Any standard book on data structures, for example Tremblay and Sorenson (1984), will give details of the range of data structures currently in use in programming languages. Such a book will also give details of the algorithm for balancing a binary tree as described in this chapter. The notion of data structures as processes arose out of the work on abstract data types which originated from work on structured programming.

CHAPTER 9

This chapter illustrates how to simulate a simple operating system in occam. Any of the standard books on operating systems mentioned above will give details of operating system functions and actions. The recent text (Tanenbaum, 1987) gives actual code for an operating system, MINIX.

CHAPTER 10

Real time systems and how to program them in occam are the subject of this chapter. A useful book on the topic of real-time systems is Freedman and Lees (1977).

CHAPTER 11

This chapter illustrates some modifications to the basic occam pairwise, synchronized communication primitive. The idea of shared channels is used in the CCS theory of Milner (Milner, 1980). The rendezvous concept was first proposed for the Ada programming language (Ada, 1980).

REFERENCES

Ada, (1982). *Reference Manual for the ADA Programming Language*, ANSI/Mil. Std. 1815A, ACM Special Publication.

Andrews, G. R. and Schneider, F. B. (1983). Concepts and notations for concurrent programming, *ACM Computing Surveys*, **15**, 3–44.

Attwood, J. W. (1976). Concurrency in operating systems, *Computer*, **9**, 18–26.

Ben-Ari, M. (1982). *Principles of Concurrent Programming*. Prentice-Hall, Englewood Cliffs.

Brinch Hansen, P. (1972). Structured Multiprogramming, *CACM*, **15**, 574–8.

Brinch Hansen, P. (1973). *Operating System Principles*. Prentice-Hall, Englewood Cliffs.

Campbell, R. and Habermann, A. (1974). The specification of process synchronisation by path expressions, *Lecture Notes in Computer Science*, **16**, Springer–Verlag, New York.

Courtois, P. J., Heymans, F. and Parnas, D. L. (1971). Concurrent control with 'readers' and 'writers'. *CACM*, **14**, 667–8.

Deitel, H. M. (1983). *An Introduction to Operation Systems*. Addison-Wesley, Wokingham.

Dijkstra, E. W. (1965). Co-operating sequential processes. In *Programming Languages*, Ed. Genuys, F. Academic Press, London and New York.

Dijkstra, E. W. (1968). The structure of the THE multiprogramming system. *CACM*, **11**, 341–6.

Dijkstra, E. W. (1971). Hierarchical ordering of sequential processes. *Acta Informatica*, **1**, 115–38.

Dijkstra, E. W. (1975). Guarded commands, non-determinacy and the formal derivation of programs. *CACM*, **18**, 453–7.

Duley, J. R. and Dietmeyer, D. L. (1968). A digital system design language (DDL), *IEEE Trans. on Computers*, **C17**, 850–61.

Flake, P. L., Moorby, P. R. and Musgrave, G. (1981). HILO Mark 2 Hardware Description Language. *Proc. 5th International Conference on Hardware Description Languages and their Applications*. Kaiserlautern, FRG.

Freedman, A. L. and Lees, R. A. (1977). *Real-time Computer Systems*. Crane Russak, New York.

Gordon, M. (1981). A very simple model of sequential behaviour of nMOS, *Proc. VLSI '81*. Edinburgh, Ed. Gray. Academic Press, London and New York.

Habermann, A. N. (1969). Prevention of system deadlocks. *CACM*, **12**, 373, 377.

Habermann, A. N. (1972). Synchronisation of communicating processes. *CACM*, **15**, 171–6.

Hanna, F. K. and Daeche, N. (1985). Specification and verification using higher order logic. *Proc. 7th Intl Symp. on CHDL and their Applications*. CHDL 85, Tokyo. Eds Koomen and Moto-oka. North Holland.

Hayes, J. P. (1986). Digital simulation with multiple logic values. *IEEE Computer Aided Design*. CAD–5, 273–83.

Hoare, C. A. R. (1972). Towards a theory of parallel programming. In *Operating System Techniques*, Ed. Hoare, C. A. R. and Perrott, R. H. Academic Press.

Hoare, C. A. R. (1974). Monitors: An operating system structuring concept. *CACM*, **17**, 549–57.

Hoare, C. A. R. (1978). Communicating sequential processes. *CACM*, **21**, 666–77.

Hoare, C. A. R. (1985). *Communicating Sequential Processes*. Prentice-Hall, Hemel Hempstead.

Holt, R. C. (1972). Some deadlock properties of computer systems. *ACM Computing Surveys*, **4**, 179–96.

Horning, J. J. and Randell, B. (1973). Process Structuring. *ACM Computing Surveys*. **5**, 5–31.

Hwang, K. and Briggs, F. A. (1984). *Computer Architecture and Parallel Processing*. McGraw-Hill, New York.

Inmos Ltd. (1984). *occam programming manual*. Prentice-Hall, Hemel Hempstead.

Isloor, S. S. and Marsland, T. A. (1980). The deadlock problem: an overview. *Computer*, **13**, 58–78.

Jones, G. (1985). Programming in 'occam'. *PRG monograph 43*. Oxford University Computing Laboratory, Oxford.

Kerridge, J. (1987). *occam programming: a practical approach*. Blackwell, Oxford.

May, D. and Shepherd, R. (1985). Occam and the transputer 19–35. In *Concurrent Languages in Distributed Systems*. Ed. Reijns, G. L. and Dagless, E. L. North Holland.

May, D. (1986). *Occam – a compiler writers guide*. Inmos Ltd.

Milne, G. J. (1985). CIRCAL and the representation of communication, concurrency and time. *ACM Trans. Prog. Lang.*, **7**, 270–98.

Milner, R. (1980). A calculus of communicating systems. *Lecture Notes in Computer Science*, **92**, Springer–Verlag, New York.

Misra, J. (1986). Distributed Discrete-Event Simulation. *A.C.M. Comp. Surveys*. **18**, 39–65.

Moszkowski, B. (1983). A temporal logic for multilevel reasoning about hardware. *Proc. 6th Intl Symp. on CHDL and their Applications*. CHDL 83, Pittsburgh, Eds Vehara and Barbacci. North Holland.

Peacock, J. K., Wong, J. W. and Manning, E. G. (1979). Distributed simulation using a network of processes. *Comput. Netw.*, **3**, 44–56.

Peterson, J. L. and Silberschatz, A. (1985). *Operating System Concepts*. Addison-Wesley, Reading, Massachusetts.

Pountain, R. and May, D. (1987). *A tutorial introduction to occam programming*. Blackwell, Oxford.

Sloman, M. and Kramer, J. (1987). *Distributed Systems and Computer Networks*. Prentice-Hall, Hemel Hempstead.

Tanenbaum, A. (1981). *Computer Networks*. Prentice-Hall, Englewood Cliffs.

Tanenbaum, A. (1987). *Operating Systems: design and implementation*. Prentice-Hall, Englewood Cliffs.

Tremblay, J.-P. and Sorenson, P. G. (1984). *An introduction to data structures with applications*. McGraw-Hill, Japan.

APPENDIX

MAJOR DIFFERENCES BETWEEN occam AND occam 2

1 **occam 2** is a typed language; standard types are INT, BYTE and BOOL. Some implementations allow REAL types also. Declarations of variables take the form as before but with one of the keywords above, for example,

```
INT fred, sum :
```

Conversions functions are provided to convert values from one type to another.

2 Channels may also be typed in occam 2, for example,

```
CHAN OF INT x :
```

Channels may carry a sequence of differently typed data and this is called a protocol. Thus a channel can be declared to carry a particular protocol, for example,

```
CHAN OF (BYTE, INT, INT)  ch :
```

which declares a channel called ch which carries data consisting of a byte quantity followed by two items of type integer. A special protocol is provided for arrays, for example, if an array i is declared as:

```
[20]INT i :
```

and a channel called pipe declared as:

```
CHAN OF (INT :: INT) pipe :
```

then the complete array may be sent down the channel by

```
pipe ! (20 :: i)
```

New types may be created by means of the TYPE declaration. This becomes especially useful for defining variant records for channels which can carry one of a number of different protocols. For example,

```
TYPE MESS IS
  CASE
    (x,INT)
    (y,BYTE)
    (z,INT,BYTE,INT)
:
```

defines a new type MESS which can represent a number of different structures each of which have a tag associated with them (x,y and z). A channel, messchan, to carry this type of information could be defined by:

```
CHAN OF MESS messchan :
```

A CASE construct is provided in occam 2 to allow for input selection, depending on which variant is sent, for example,

```
CASE messchan ?
  (x,i1)
    .. process
  (y,ch)
    .. process
  (z,i1,ch,i2)
    .. process
```

where i1 and i2 have been declared as integers and ch as a byte. The CASE construct can be included in an ALT construct to wait on an input channel.

3 Multi-dimensional arrays are possible in occam 2. For example,a 2-D array of bytes called display would be declared by, say,

```
[8][7] BYTE display :
```

and values assigned to the elements by assignment processes such as:

```
display[2][2] := 4
```

(Note: this removes some of the difficulties of programming the crossbar switch and courier examples of Chapter 5.)

These are just the major changes in occam 2; there are a large number of minor changes, such as changes in the syntax of some of the constructs. In fact, as this is being written, changes are still being made to the definition of occam 2, although the main features of the language have been established for some time. Interested readers should consult the book given in the references.

INDEX